Jack B-C
DOGSTAR

Jill Marshall

Jill Marshall Books
First published by Jill Marshall books 2020
Copyright © Jill Marshall

The right of Jill Marshall to be identified as the author of this work has been asserted by her in accordance with the Copyright, Designs and Patents Act 1988.

All rights reserved. No part of this publication may be reproduced, stored in or introduced into a retrieval system, or transmitted, in any form, or by any means (electronic, mechanical, photocopying, recording or otherwise) without the prior written permission of the publisher. Any person who does any unauthorized act in relation to this publication may be liable to criminal prosecution and civil claims for damages.

A CIP catalogue record for this book is available from the National Library of New Zealand

ISBN **978-1-99-002450-4 Paperback**
Cover Design by Katie Gannon
Illustrations by Madison Fotti-Knowles

This book is sold subject to the condition that it shall not, by way of trade or otherwise, be lent, resold, hired out, or otherwise circulated without the publisher's prior consent in any form of binding or cover other than that in which it is published and without a similar condition including this condition being imposed on the subsequent purchaser.

For my grandparents. Now I'm one myself,
I know what it truly means.
You are stars in my forever now.
xxx

Chapter 1

Jack Bootle-Cadogan pulled his backpack out from under his bed and tipped the contents out all over the floor.

'Maths, English, Chemistry,' he muttered, frowning in concentration as he stowed the books back in order. It was a mighty frown indeed, consisting of one hairy monobrow topped by a thatch of blue-black hair. 'Social sciences, two books ... where are they ... yep, got them. Drama – yuck. PE, double yuck.'

It was only yuck because of Guisely, the PE teacher who must have been Hitler in a past life. Other than that, thought Jack as he stuffed his shorts into the miniscule space left by his files, he was actually enjoying sports. Basketball was great, especially hanging out with Fraser and even Minty. Running was fantastic, as he aced it every time. Even football was turning into a possibility now that he'd mastered the skill of dribbling – or rather, of not dribbling, all over the ball with his great, lolling tongue. Not trying to nudge it with his nose or fling it around between his teeth. Football season was just about to begin anew as the school year began, and Jack actually felt quite encouraged. He might even try out for the Clearwell Comp team this time around ...

Now that the bag was crammed to capacity, Jack leapt to his feet and stretched out to his full height before the mirror. He'd been forced to raise the mirror a full half metre in the last couple of months, and not just because he was having your average teenage growth spurt. No, the future Lord Jack Bootle-Cadogan, or Jack B-C to his friends (and occasionally Doghead to his really, really good friends) was having the growth spurt to end all spurts. On a nightly basis he turned into the Egyptian God of Mummification and General Death, exchanging his normal gangly teen limbs for the muscular power-tools of a deity, and his frothy mop of hair for a covering of black fur that bristled all over his head and right down to his collar bone.

It was this head that stared back at him in the mirror.

'Go away, stupid fur,' said Jack mournfully.

As his own voice projected from inside it, the black-lipped snout in his reflection parted to demonstrate a great set of pointy fangs and a large flappy tongue. He stuck the tongue out in disgust, then felt even more revolted as it connected with the mirror's surface and deposited a sickly trail of saliva up the glass. 'Nooo,' he groaned. 'Bone, please help.'

But Bone wasn't there.

For the first time ever in Jack's living memory, their trusted family retainer, Bone, was not on hand to help him get ready for school. True, Jack was a bit old to need nurse-maiding, but still, it was tradition: Bone packed his bag (it was the first time Jack had done it himself on the opening day of the term); Bone laid out his uniform (first time he'd done this himself too, only to discover it wasn't ironed); Bone (apparently) ironed his uniform ready for Jack to scrumple it up again, and then Bone prodded him into getting to breakfast on time before taking him to Clearwell in the Daimler.

In recent months he'd been even more useful: since the family curse that turned him into Anubis had been revived on the death of Jack's great-grandmother, Bone had also proven himself to be a dab hand with the cut-throat razor and had managed to make Jack look at least a bit normal on the odd day his dog-face was still hanging around in the morning.

It was his own fault, of course, that Bone wasn't there any longer. During the unfolding of their adventures about being cursed, they had discovered that Bone was actually Albert Cornthwaite, scientist/archeologist and explorer, and assistant to Lord Jay B-C when he discovered the tomb of Osiris. Not only that, but Al-Bone's family were the village undertakers. When Jack's father, the current Lord B-C, had started getting funny about servants living in estate houses for free, Jack had discovered a way to let Bone out of his arrangement with the Bootle-Cadogans. He had moved into the undertakers' cottage, set up his own business dealing with death, and at the same time begun his own life.

Jack missed him.

His father missed Bone too, although he wouldn't admit it. Jack's mother told him she missed Bone because her husband was a grouch without his soft-boiled egg in the morning, and because she could see how bereft Lord Jackson was without Bone around as he had been throughout his life. Everybody seemed a little sadder without Bone lurching round corners on his spindly legs, eyeballing terrified National Trust staff with his strange violet corneas and inclining his white skull of a head left and right in place of speaking, like a wobbly-headed garden gnome.

Which was why Jack was very surprised when someone knocked at the door and then entered without waiting for Jack to say anything.

'Bone!' He spun around and dropped the towel he'd been trying to wrap around his muzzle in case it was a member of staff, or worse still, one of his parents. 'What are you doing here?'

Formally dressed in his undertaking outfit (a black suit very like the one he'd worn for his work at Lowmount Hall), Bone flashed his purple eyes at Jack. He flung his hands up in the air in the most violent of shrugs. 'Sir,' he bellowed.

'Ah.' Jack had spent a lifetime interpreting Bone-mime, so he knew exactly what this meant. 'You don't know why you're here,' he interpreted quickly, 'and you'd really rather not be here at all.'

Bone folded his arms truculently.

'Well, it's not my fault,' said Jack. 'I didn't ask you to come. Although as you're here, ahem, would you mind, ahem, removing my dog face?'

He wished he'd re-phrased that. His friend and erstwhile butler looked as though he'd relish the opportunity to remove Jack's dog face, completely severing it from his dog shoulders by slicing through his dog neck. 'Please?' bleated Jack, frankly a little scared.

Bone gave him a long stare, clearly trying to work out if he had the energy or the mime-moves to shout, 'Do it yourself, you lazy git! Remember? Me not stupid servant any more!' Then he sighed and jerked his head towards the chair, which Jack took as invitation to get his face shaved off.

While they avoided each other's eyes either side of the cut-throat razor, Jack's brain went into overtime. Why was Bone here? He clearly didn't want to be. Come to think of it, why was Jack's Anubis head hanging around after Ra had risen in the sky (or the sun was up, as most people would put it)?

In fact, why was it that he could never just go to school, get his lunch money thumped out of his pockets (possibly by Minty), be psychologically abused by Guisely, several pupils and a couple of other teachers and then come home starving, filthy, worn out and wondering if he'd learned anything whatsoever that day?

Why, in other words, couldn't his first day of the new school year be *normal*?

This wasn't normal. Even for him, it wasn't normal. He waited until Bone had circumnavigated his Adam's apple and then said, 'Something's up.'

Bone tutted. 'You think?' said his tut.

'Yeah. You're not meant to be here any more but now that I think about it, I did ask you to come. I shouted aloud for your help. Not that I really want it!' he added hastily. 'Did you ... were you, like, called?'

As he wiped the razor blade on a small white towel, every inch like Sweeney Todd, Bone gave a curt nod. He acted out being dragged along by an invisible force in a way that would have made anyone else think he was doing zombie impressions, but which caused Jack to be alarmed for other reasons.

'The curse. It's still got a hold over you. The Bootle-Cadogans serve Seth as the God of Death and stuff, and you serve the Bootle-Cadogans.'

Looking less angry and more concerned now, Bone nodded, perching on the edge of the bed as he waved at Jack to continue.

'And that would explain why I still have my Anubis head.'

Jack studied his face in the mirror. Blue-black stubble was already beginning to sweep across his cheeks, and his eyebrows were busily knitting themselves back together.

'I'm sorry to ask, Bone, but I think we need to meet in the crypt,' he said at length.

It would probably make him late for school, but he couldn't go like this, and anyway, "late" was the only good time to get to Clearwell Comp. On time meant *geek*, and *geek* meant beaten up. Meeting in the crypt meant that he and his friend could talk, as Bone would be restored to his young self, Albie Cornthwaite.

To his relief, Bone simply said, 'Sir,' in a resigned tone of voice, before backing silently out through the door.

It was still early. Jack's parents would only just be getting into breakfast and beginning their morning ritual of contented sniping at each other over the newspapers. Breakfast was the only meal they were guaranteed to have together. Since Jack had opened the great money-pit of a stately home to the public as holiday lets with spa pools, life had been much sweeter for them financially, but they were so busy all summer that they didn't know themselves half the time. Jack checked his watch. If he was quick - and clever with some disguises - he could grab a piece of toast with them for two minutes before heading off to Clearwell.

Pulling on his dressing gown, Jack yanked up the hood and padded softly from his room. To his astonishment, however, his mother appeared suddenly from her own bedroom, closing the door firmly behind her. She spotted Jack who had frozen in the corridor. 'Your father's having a lie-in,' she said. 'Don't disturb him.'

'Wouldn't dream of it,' Jack mumbled from the depths of his hood.

'Why aren't you dressed? Honestly,' she snapped, brushing past him en route to the dining room, 'you're as bad as your father. A few weeks without Bone doing everything for you and you can't even manage to get up in the morning.'

'Yes. It's true. Fair point,' said Jack. Anything to keep her quiet. Keep her moving. Keep her out of his way.

'You'll be late for Prison. I mean, school.'

'Yes. No! Be there in a minute.'

His mother flapped a hand in the air. 'It's your funeral. I don't even care. Time to grow up, Jack, and start looking after yourself.'

If only you knew, he thought darkly as she stomped away. If Jack grew any more he'd be in the Guinness Book of Records, and as for looking after himself – well, he did that and much, much more. Even so, Jack was very glad that Bone hadn't been around to hear that exchange. Reminded of his mission, he sped up towards the museum.

'Meeting in the Crypt,' he called to the two figures parked either side of Granny Dazzle's fabulous display of Egyptian jewellery, one statue holding a bowl of water on her head and the other with arms crossed over his athletic chest, a flail in one hand and a crook in the other. He wasn't the only one who'd grown. They were taller too, he noticed – no longer the young children he'd met just a few months ago, but now young adults like him. How had they aged so much in such a short time? That was the way with gods, he supposed.

'Ozzy! Ice!' he shouted, rousing them from their stasis. 'Get a move on; I've got to go to school.'

With a tiny tremor, the female yawned delicately and then smiled at Jack. 'Ra in you, dear Jack,' she said.

'In you Ra, dear Isis,' he returned. Jack wasn't at all sure if that was what he was meant to say, but as this was how Ice and Ozzy spoke all the time, like godly Yodas, he knew he wouldn't be far off.

Ozzy – a.k.a. Osiris, god of agriculture and green stuff – seemed to approve. As Jack watched, the green statue that had stood before him just seconds ago shimmered into life as the figure breathed in and out. 'Yeh, Jack. We have meeting?'

'Meeting we have. I thought we'd broken the curse, but it looks as though Bone's still under orders from the B-Cs, which might mean—'

He didn't need to say it. The Bootle-Cadogans could still be under orders from Seth, the evil god who had murdered Osiris once already, and now fancied doing it one more time since Isis sought out his scattered body parts and attempted to put him back together again.

Jack glanced at his friends. Quite often, by now, Ice would be wailing and Ozzy might have paled into a light green sweat, like Jack's father with a hangover. This time, however, they were just staring at each other with granite eyes. Ice's, especially, were as hard as chips of sapphire. They were definitely growing up fast, getting stronger in every way.

'Could you call Minty?' he said softly, reluctant to interrupt whatever invisible, inaudible conversation they were having with their matching stony stares.

'Done,' said Ice without hesitation.

'Good. Then, errr, let's go.'

Heading across the museum to the wall inscribed with a large Eye of Horus, Jack seized the door knob in the pupil of the eye and yanked open the door. He stood back politely as Ozzy and Ice floated past him along the corridor before following them along the sandy floor. Taller. Definitely taller – they all were. Once they'd barely reached halfway up the walls; now all three had to bend their heads slightly to fit inside the underground passage. It was quite a relief to reach the door at the far end without a crick in his doggy neck.

Entering behind Ice, Jack found Bone sitting on the stone steps leading to the altar, in his young incarnation as Albie Cornthwaite. Beside him sat Minty, her hawk positioned on her knee from where he was keeping a keen eye on the mice scrabbling around the candle niches. This was probably to help Minty, the goddess Amentet, keep a clear head, as Hathor could install images in her brain with his bird's eye viewpoint. Minty's hair, Jack noticed suddenly, was especially black and shiny today, like a very sleek crash-helmet. Like she'd just washed it. Like she'd … made an effort?

Eugh. Why was he even thinking about her hair? She was a girl. A girl who hated him. And a … a girl. Glad that she couldn't read minds, Jack nodded to Minty and side-stepped her carefully so she couldn't casually take his feet out from under him, which was her latest favourite past-time.

Ozzy and Ice had taken up their customary positions on either end of Granny Dazzle's sarcophagus, so Jack now jumped up into the space between them.

'There's something funny going on today,' he said.

'Yeah, first day of school. Are you scared?' Minty grinned nastily at him.

'No. Well, yes, a little, but not of school.'

Albie stood up. 'I think Jack's right,' he said. 'You know the Seth curse about B-Cs serving him and me serving them? We thought we'd broken it at the water park,' – where they'd blasted Seth into a million droplets – 'because I was able to take over the undertakers and there haven't been any problems. This morning, however, I heard a cry for help from the Hall.' From behind his round-framed spectacles, Albie's eyes flashed at Jack. 'And I was compelled to assist. Literally,' he added. 'My feet marched me along to the car and then my hands steered me to the Hall, and then it was marchy march all the way to Master Jack's bedroom.'

'You needed help, Jack?' Osiris asked.

He waved a hand. 'Nooooo. Not really. Just one of those things you say. But … Well, I do have to go back to school today and I woke up with this,' Jack said, pointing at his muzzle. 'It hasn't happened during the day since June 21st, - you know, the solstice when we tackled the Pig last time. So I figured there must be something wrong.'

Ozzy and Ice were doing flinty stares at each other again, and Minty was joining in. Minty the Flinty. With the shiny hair. Hair that probably smelt nice.

Seriously, what was wrong with him?

'You two,' said Jack, ignoring the fact that Minty was clearly in on it too. 'What's going on?'

'It is a new year for you, Jack, yes?' said Ozzy, leaning thoughtfully on his crook.

'A new year it is.'

Ice nodded. 'In our world, it is a new year too. Since Sirius the Dogstar rose bright in the sky it is the season of Ahket, the inundation. This is the time of Osiris.'

'The Nile floods and the land is fertile, bringing health and food and prosperity to the united lands of bees and sedge,' said Osiris humbly, as if it wasn't all his doing and it just happened by accident. 'If I am not restored to full strength, great damage will be done.'

'It's Ma'at, Jack,' said Minty. He glanced at her in shock. Sometimes he found it hard to remember that she was an Egyptian goddess too, rather than a very big pain in his human behind. Or even his canine one. 'Ma'at is the natural order of things. Without order, there is chaos.'

'Chaos there is,' echoed Ice. 'And order must be returned.'

Albie coughed politely. 'So if I'm understanding you correctly,' he said, 'all sorts of chaos is about to be unleashed on the world unless the correct order is put back in place.'

Ozzy and Ice nodded as one.

'Which means Osiris has to be restored to full power, Seth has to be defeated, and Anubis has to get on with doing his job properly.'

Again they nodded. 'It is Ma'at,' the trio intoned together.

'It sounds to me, Jack,' said Albie, 'as if you have to make a choice. Here or … or there.'

The three gods all grinned happily. 'Here or there,' and 'There or here' and 'Easy, huh?' said Ozzy, Ice and Minty in turn.

Jack stared at them all, and then shook his head. 'No way. I'm not disappearing into the Field of Rushes for all eternity, embalming people forever.'

'Then that leaves only one choice,' said Albie. 'We have to remove the curse and free you from your responsibilities.'

'And you, too,' said Jack.

Albie nodded. 'Yes. And me too.'

That was all that needed doing, then – removing a curse from two families and restoring one Egyptian god to full power while disposing of another particularly evil one. It was laughable, how easy everyone else always assumed these little tasks were going to be.

But just as Jack started to ask, 'And how are we going to do that?' Ice's chilling voice rang out across the crypt.

'It is time!' she cried. 'Time it is. Time for the undoing!'

Jack gulped. He wasn't quite sure why, but being undone sounded a whole lot more painful than being ... well, done. Created. Especially when he had not the faintest clue how to go about it.

Still, now he was *totally* late for school, so maybe he'd get a preview of what it felt like to be undone. Especially as his face would be furred over again.

'Great,' said Jack despondently. 'Cursed by Seth, and cursed by Guisely.'

'It's Ma'at, Jack,' said Minty again, only this time with a nasty grin. 'The natural order of things.'

'With me at the bottom of the pile.'

Minty just shrugged, and snuffed out the candles.

Chapter 2

'The thing is,' Jack admitted to Albie, once they were on their own, 'I suppose in some ways I quite like being a god. I'm not sure I want to give it up.'

Albie raised one eyebrow sardonically. 'Sure. What's not to like? Super-human strength. Excellent hearing.'

'Running like a greyhound, only faster.'

'Having adventures that would have made Jay the famous adventurer jealous,' continued Albie.

'Zipping!' splurted Jack, suddenly remembering his amazing ability to slide through objects and even people at immense velocity, just by thinking about where he wanted to go. 'Zipping is outstanding.'

He'd drifted off into a reverie when he realised that Albie was adding his own items to the list: ordering people around; summoning servants just by saying their name; chatting to the ghosts of dead relatives …

Jack tuned in properly just as Albie was droning, 'Hanging out with other gods in the Hall of Judgement and the Field of Rushes. Never having to worry about making a living—'

'I will have to make a living,' he said quickly. 'Even if I was a god, I'd have to make money in this world.'

'But you're a lord,' Albie pointed out.

'Not yet.'

It was what he dreaded the most – the day he'd have to announce that he was Lord Bootle-Cadogan of Lowmount. Thankfully it was still a long way off, and he'd managed to avoid the traditional lordly customs of going to Eton and then into merchant banking or the army.

So far.

'Anyway, lords aren't all rich. You've seen how broke my parents are. I might have to sell the castle or something.'

'Sell Lowmount?' Albie leapt to his feet, outraged. 'Over my dead body. Sell Diselda's resting place, and the estate where I grew up and met Jay, where I—'

'Okay, okay,' said Jack quickly. 'I won't sell it!'

'Promise?'

Jack laughed, shaking his head. 'Look, you're getting your bandages in a bunch over nothing. My dad is still the lord, and he's such a stickler for tradition that there's no way he'd ever sell Lowmount.'

Albie was still staring at him mutinously, his hand stuck out rigidly as he waited for Jack to shake on a deal. 'Promise me, Jack.'

Well, what difference did it make? Jack took the iron fingers and shook them, then held out his hand again, palm upwards and thumb stretched apart from his fingers. 'Promise,' he said. 'And these days we sort of clasp hands around our thumbs, and slap each other's back.'

'I've seen that at your school.' Albie scowled. 'I'm not doing it.'

'It won't be a proper promise otherwise. It's the 21st century, Albie.'

'No way.' Albie tucked his thumbs into his armpits.

'Okay. No promise then,' said Jack airily.

Finally, Albie snapped. 'All right! Do your stupid hand grip. Just ... get on with it.'

Having goaded him into it, it didn't seem much fun to taunt Albie and his old-fashioned ideals any more. In Anubis form, Jack was a good head taller than his friend; he stood awkwardly and pulled Albie towards him with his curled fist, patting him gently between the shoulder blades. Any harder and Albie might snap, so thin was he, and so over-powered was Jack. As he felt the bony outline of Albie's ribs beneath his thin jacket, Jack suddenly realised what was behind all his remonstrations.

'I'll look after you, Albie,' he said quietly. 'Whatever happens. Whether I'm a god or a lord or just an ordinary person, I'll make sure you have a home and a ... a family. Even if it's just me.'

'That's what your great-grandfather promised me too,' said Albie sourly, but he glanced at Jack. 'But thank you,' he added, so quietly that Jack could only just hear it.

'No problem.'

He headed outside, only to find Minty lying in wait for him ready to give him 'stop being a dog god' lessons on the steps of the crypt, while Albie-Bone texted Jack's mother to excuse him from breakfast and limped off to get the

Daimler. And Jack's uniform. And his bag. Just like old times ...

'I told you, moron, you just have to concentrate. FOcus,' rapped Minty, tapping her temple to show him just exactly what was wrong with him.

'I am focussing. I only stop focussing because you keep talking to me.'

She gazed at him with an odd expression, somewhere between frustration and laughter. 'Why do I bother?'

'Because you're an interfering cow and you can't help yourself?' Jack ducked to avoid a jab to his throat and caught it in the eye instead. 'Ow. It was just a thought.'

'Don't think,' said Minty, scowling. 'Focus. I am a human. I am a human.'

'You are a human. You are a human.'

'No, dufus. I, Jack B-C, am a human.'

'Oh. Right.'

He tried again and this time it did seem to work. For at least a minute and a half he was Jack, teenage boy - lanky, scruffy, possibly curly-haired although he couldn't see, and not sure what to do with his limbs. Then the moment he wondered if he'd changed completely and put a hand to his face to check, he morphed back to Anubis.

'Focus, and LOCK!' snarled Minty. 'Focus and LOCK!'

Thankfully, Jack could hear the distant thrum of the Daimler's V8 engine. If he focussed and LOCKED on that he could be in the passenger seat in half a second flat.

'Come on, Jack, you can do it. I know you can!' Minty was shouting at him now. 'I, Jack BC, am a human. Focus, lock and BE YOURSELF!'

'I, Jack BC, am a human. Focus and LOCK. Be ... Be myself? Why would I want to do that?'

Minty stared at him in utter disgust. 'What was I ever thinking?' she muttered, almost to herself. 'You're hopeless. Completely hopeless.'

'Sorry,' he said with a small nod. 'It's true.'

'But Jack, you ...' Minty started. Then she seemed to think better of it. 'Nothing. See you at school. I'll make us not late.' She could do that by creating a rainfall and turning back time for a few minutes.

So he wasn't too late for school, at least. And if he did what Minty had suggested he could manage to stay in his human form for much of the time. It was only when he got interested in the lesson and began listening to the teacher that his focus slipped and he could feel his ears expanding through this hair - or when he got nervous.

Nervous, of course, was what he was around Guisely. Somehow the nasty rodent of a teacher knew exactly how to push his buttons. Jack had never worked out why Guisely disliked him so much, other than the fact that he was one day going to be a lord etcetera. It wasn't his fault. Nonetheless, dislike him he did, and Guisely lost no opportunity to drive it home to him.

'Spend the holidays playing polo, did we, Posh?' the teacher sneered as Jack skulked into the sports hall.

'Cleaning holiday lets, actually, Sir,' said Jack. *I'm a human, I'm a human, I'm a human.*

'Oh, that's right. Letting the great unwashed stay at the palace. Not enough servants to go around, then?'

'We don't have servants, Mr Guisely,' said Jack, gritting his teeth. *Not that old chestnut again. I'm a human, I'm a human.*

Guisely favoured him with his yellow rat grin. 'Well, run along. Looks like your girlfriend's waiting for you.'

I, Jack BC, am a human. Focus and LOCK. I, Jack BC, am a human ... 'Girlfriend, sir?'

'Miss West over there, waving at you to join her.' While he was nodding across the hall, Guisely caught a glimpse of something else. 'WHAT is wrong with your neck? Talk about the great unwashed!'

Miss West? Minty? 'I, Jack BC, am a human. Focus and LOCK!'

Oh good lord. He'd said it aloud. He knew it - from the look on Guisely's face and the sniggers from all around him, and from the way Minty closed her eyes in despair, able to hear him all the way across the other side of the hall with her Amentet powers.

Overpowering Jack with breath so evil that he could have taken on Seth in a stench contest, Guisely leaned in close. 'You get weirder every year, Posh with Dosh. I suggest that you make this the year of keeping out of my way.'

'Oh, that's every year, sir,' murmured Jack, nodding, but Guisely had lost interest and moved on to his next victim. Minty, meanwhile, just glared at him and shook her head very, very slowly...

Throughout the rest of the day, Jack managed to keep his head in place by staying completely silent and staring at a spot just above the eyebrows of whichever teacher was at the front of the room. It took so much effort that he started to sweat, and by the time he'd given up all pretence at being able to manage, his uniform felt like a damp sponge. He was almost relieved to see Guisely pressing his ugly face to the panes of glass in the door as it gave him a second to stop straining his eyeballs. Then his heart sank. The man was searching for someone's face. His face. Spotting Jack, he cocked his head towards the corridor.

'No matter how many times I tell you,' said Guisely, hoisting up his belt so that his trousers lifted a full ten centimetres above his socks, 'and no matter how many times you insist that you don't have them, it appears that Lord Fancy Pants just can't stop his servants turning up at the school.'

Jack zoned in on the greasy crease between Guisely's eyebrows. *Focussy focus. Human human human.* 'Someone's here for me. Who... is it the ... erm ... driver?' He didn't like to mention Bone's name aloud in case his friend and ally suddenly slithered into the corridor against his will.

'I hope not. He's younger than you. Child slavery day at the castle, is it?' Guisely sniggered nastily.

'No, sir. Honestly. It never is.'

It must be Ozzy, somehow small and paler green again ... which would all take some clever tactical avoidance but was better than Bone playing Involuntary Frankenstein through the fields of Clearwell Comp.

But then Guisely abruptly stuck out an arm and yanked the visitor forward from behind a stationery cupboard. Jack felt his chest fill with relief. It wasn't one of his friends. He'd never seen this boy before in his life.

'There's been a mistake,' he said, smiling at the boy who stared at him, startled round eyes glowing against his dark skin. 'Sorry. Who was it you were looking for?'

The boy's curly eyelashes fluttered as he heard Jack's voice, and then, to Jack's complete mystification, he laughed aloud.

'Lord Bootle-Cadogan, it IS you!' said the younger kid. 'I am so happy to see you again!'

Guisely's lip curled. 'Not yours? Mistake? I'll tell you what the mistake is ...'

'No, sir, honestly,' said Jack quickly, guessing immediately that the mistake would feature Jack himself in any number of roles. 'I don't know him. I don't know you,' he repeated to the boy himself.

At first the boy frowned, perplexed, but then his face relaxed into a broad, beaming smile. 'Oh, Master, you are always liking to play the jokes on me!'

'No, I'm not ...' Blimey, this was going to be a hard one to wriggle out of. Guisely folded his arms and leaned against the wall, smug as anything, settling in to enjoy the show. 'I'm so sorry, but we really haven't met before. And I'm not your master, either.'

The frown returned. 'You do sound a little different, it is true,' said the boy, delving into a pocket sewn into the side of his long white African robe. 'And absolutely you are younger than I expected. But then ... so am I!' He laughed again, his mighty smile lighting up the corridor.

'Definitely one of yours,' muttered the teacher. 'Talks rubbish, just like you.'

'You're mixing me up with someone else,' said Jack firmly. 'We've never met, and to be honest, you're not making a whole lot of sense.'

But then he saw the newspaper clipping that the boy was holding out, and his breath caught in this throat. It was a photograph he'd seen before, and he could see why the boy had been confused.

The picture showed Albie in his favoured archaeologist's suit – pale ochre trousers and a wafting white shirt - watching stiffly as a coffin was raised from the ground. Beside him, directing operations, stood a man who did look rather like Jack – which was not all that surprising since he was Jack's ancestor. His great-grandfather, in fact.

The boy had mistaken him for Lord Jay.

But that had been almost a hundred years ago, so of course Jay wouldn't be that young now. He would, in fact, be dead. Obviously.

Funnily enough, though, while Lord Jay Bootle-Cadogan was indeed dead, the two other people in the photo were not. Albert Cornthwaite lived on as the albino butler, Bone. And the other person in the picture, standing beneath the tilting coffin as it was levered towards the ground with their head tipped back and a broad grin across his face, was somehow still alive too.

Very alive. And right there in front of him, in the science corridor of Clearwell Comp.

'I ... yes, I remember now,' stuttered Jack, hardly able to think clearly at all but knowing beyond a shadow of a doubt that he couldn't start explaining here, in front of a teacher who'd already seen far too much for anyone's comfort. 'I'd better ... better take you back to Lowmount.'

'Ah, thank you, Lord B-C! To your castle! I would be most honoured.'

Guisely looked about ready to vomit, so Jack simply gripped the boy by the shoulder and slid him along the corridor until they reached the toilets. 'Thanks, sir! I'll get him home now.'

Guisely called after him. 'Do us all a favour, and don't come back.'

'No, I'll be back! See you later!'

He slid them both into the changing room and spun around to confront the boy.

'This is you, in the picture?'

The boy guffawed heartily. 'Yes! And you, Lord Jay.'

'That's just it,' squeaked Jack. 'I'm not Lord Jay – I'm Lord Jack. I mean, Jack.'

'You are not Lord Jay? This is not a joke?' The boy looked utterly crestfallen. 'But I come all this way to find him and Master Cornthwaite. Where is Lord Jay?'

'He ... he died, not long after this photo was taken,' said Jack.

The great dark eyes filled with tears. 'That is what I am told, but after what happened to me I hope that it is not true – that the two masters live as I do!'

'But that's just it,' said Jack swiftly. 'Jay died, but Albie Cornthwaite *is* still alive – sort of and sometimes, and mostly as an ancient old git.'

'Master Cornthwaite is alive! Ah, praise Re and Nut, that is good to hear, for I have disturbing news for him.'

'Well, that figures. It's usually disturbing news when someone turns up looking like a teenager when they should be – what, 110 years old?'

'I am one hundred and eight years old, Lord Jack,' said the boy proudly.

'Not Lord, it's just Jack.'

'Master Jack?'

'Okay, if you must.' Jack sighed. 'So can you explain why haven't aged? Was it a curse, like Bone – I mean, Albie?'

The boy raised his hands to the roof. 'A curse?' His laughter rolled around the empty lavatories. 'No, Master Jack, it is the opposite of a curse. It is a miracle! I swim in the waters of Abydos, my friend. I submerge myself in the fountain of youth delivered from the great Osiris himself, and so I stay as young as the moment when I enter that churning and terrifying lake.' He grinned as if he'd just described a day out at a funfair.

Jack stared him up and down, taking in the youthful appearance that contrasted so strongly with the aged being that Bone had become. 'You've been like this for nearly a century?'

'Yes. And while it is a blessed miracle that occurs to me, mine is being a curious and sometimes lonely life, having to leave my family behind as they grow older and I do not.'

'I understand. And Albie-Bone will get it completely.'

The boy's eyes blinked sadly. 'So I must tell Master Cornthwaite of my distressful news,' he said suddenly.

'Oh! That wasn't it? I thought your news was that you'd managed to stay fourteen this whole time.'

'No, indeed, Master Jack, it is much more disturberous than that. Until a couple of days ago I am, as you say, the exact same age as when I swim at Abydos. In the last two days, though, I am getting older. A year older, I would suggest, with each passing day.'

Jack sucked in a breath. That didn't sound good. It sounded the opposite of good, in fact – as if the natural order that had been maintained for nearly a hundred years was beginning to fall apart.

Just as Ozzy and Ice had said.

'I think,' he said gently, 'that it's time we reintroduced you to Master Cornthwaite.'

He called for Bone and the friend-butler appeared within minutes; he still seemed to be forced to do Jack's bidding. The purple eyes bulged at the sight of Jack's companion, before filling with tears as the boy's had done earlier.

Jack watched the two of them pointing at the photo and then at each other's faces, nodding and gasping as Bone gurgled madly in the back of his throat and the boy cried, 'Master Cornthwaite! Why you are not young like me? How does this happen?'

'Take us home, Bone,' he said after a few moments. 'Drop me off at the big house and then get your friend to the crypt where you can catch up properly. I'll see you there in about an hour.'

Bone nodded happily, clapping the young man so firmly between the shoulder-blades that he almost shoved him through the toilet stalls. Jack extracted him from the loo roll holder and led the way to the car.

He clambered silently into the back of the Daimler, wondering just what this new development meant?

One thing was certain. Everything was about to change.

Again.

Chapter 3

It seemed curiously quiet at home, even for an enormous, echoey castle.

'Hello?' he called softly, only to find his mother racing to the door to meet him.

'Shhhhh!' She seemed unusually agitated. 'Your father's still in bed. Don't wake him up - you know what a terrible mood he gets in.'

'Still in bed?'

'He's got a cold,' said his mother. 'Making it out to be pneumonia. You know what he's like.'

He did, and he was about to smile when he caught the worried expression behind his mother's smile. She was concerned – more than she was admitting. 'Is he asleep?'

Jack's mother nodded. 'Probably something to do with the whiskey he's been medicating himself with. I'm just going to order some more.'

She trailed away disconsolately, off to her beloved laptop where Roger would lie on her feet and where access to the outside world was readily available.

Her tone worried him. As soon as she was out of sight, Jack allowed himself to de-focus into godly status and immediately imagined the enormous mahogany wardrobe in his parents' room. Zip! Within seconds he had sliced through walls as if they were mist and slipped into the back of the wardrobe among the winter coats. Feeling like someone about to enter Narnia in reverse, he opened the door to spy on his father.

Jackson Bootle-Cadogan was asleep, it was true, but it wasn't his usual snoring and snorting, energetic sort of a sleep, like a stamping stallion. He was quiet and still, every breath long and … thin, somehow. It occurred to Jack that his father seemed smaller than usual. A little frail. A frail old man. And for the first time in his life, Jack realised that his father wasn't only unusual because he was a lord. He was unusual because he was very much older than all his friends' dads.

Jack wondered, actually, how old his father was. Maybe he hadn't escaped the curse at all. Maybe he was centuries old, like Bone, and had never told Jack.

He would have to ask him, when he was better. Right now, he looked like a sick child needing sleep. From the other side of the bed, a figure formed mostly from vapour shimmied raised a hand in Jack's direction. Granny Dazzle. What was she doing here? At first he thought she was waving, but then he saw that she was putting a finger to her lips. He could almost hear her whisper rustling through the clothes in the wardrobe: Shshshshshshshshsh.

Feeling strangely out-of-sorts, Jack pulled the wardrobe door closed. Now wasn't the time to be disturbing his father – or his mother, or his ghostly great-grandmother who was clearly very busy. He remembered Granny Dazzle's gentle 'hush' and sighed along with it. He felt like some peace, too; somewhere quiet to get his head – heads – straight. A thinking spot.

All at once he identified the perfect place, and he conjured it in his mind's eye: a tree, broad-trunked and whispering, out beyond the fence that surrounded the crypt. The wardrobe instantly separated into atoms, followed by the wall and the entire wing of the castle and the gardens as Jack was spirited to Granny Dazzle's favourite place. Throughout his whole life she'd painted beneath its leaves, or scribbled there in her journal, or simply stared out over the pastures towards the forest. It was her tree. Jack felt quite ashamed that he'd abandoned it – he hadn't even visited it since the day of her funeral when his peculiar adventures had begun.

Now he touched the bark, wondering what it was about it that had given Granny Dazzle so much comfort. It was a nice tree, for sure, but he didn't feel anything unusual about it. Diselda must simply have liked the shade, and the broad expanse to lean upon.

Jack flopped down onto the grass, pressing his back up against the gnarled and knotted trunk. 'What would you do, Granny's tree?' he said softly. 'How would you tackle Seth and his disruption of the natural order of things?'

As soon as the words left his mouth, an earthquake jolted through the ground beneath him and he felt the tree transforming against his spine. At once he realised that there was nothing normal about this tree. Jack turned around in dread, sure that the spitting face of a venomous pig-god was bound to be slavering at him.

And he was right: there *was* a face there, imprinted in the whorls across the bark, shaped by the knots and gnarly outcrops into the beautiful smile of a goddess.

'It is time,' said the face in a voice so golden that Jack felt his hands turn to liquid.

He smiled nervously. 'People keep telling me that.'

The face frowned in fury. 'Now it is time, Anubis. Time it is.'

'Time for what? Undoing?'

'For this,' said the voice.

Beneath her face, the bark shifted and rearranged itself into a flattened plaque covered by a series of images that Jack recognised as Egyptian hieroglyphs. He could even recognise himself among the pictures – Anubis … and Ozzy, and Ice, and the pig-faced Seth, all attacking each other with crooks and flails and snake-headed sticks in a seemingly random fashion which nobody was going to win. To one side stood a woman – a goddess. Jack peered at her face. It was the same as the one emblazoned into the tree trunk above the plaque.

'I can't read Egyptian,' he said in despair. 'What's that supposed to mean?'

The barky face swivelled towards him. 'In your language then,' cried the goddess.

'Sister helps sister,
Brother fights brother,

Sons honour fathers -
Ma'at is forever.'

'Great. A rhyme,' said Jack, smiling weakly. 'I should have known there'd be a rhyme.'

The face raised an eyebrow at him. 'Is there a problem with that, Anubis?'

'Nope. No, that's fine.'

The woman smiled then, and Jack was suddenly reminded of Ice when she stopped being chilly – or crying a lot. 'Sorry to ask, but ... who are you?'

'The sister of the bark,' said the face. 'The other sister.'

'Sister helps sister,' repeated Jack. 'So you're ...'

Just as he was wondering whose sister she was, the face swirled like a whirlpool and closed down. Beneath the knobble of wood on which the goddess had appeared, the hieroglyphs leapt around in a frenzy, the bark bubbling and erupting like lava, so violently that splinters and chips began to fly off the tree trunk. A sizeable chunk split away from the tree with a horrendous screech and shot out of the tree towards Jack, missing his eye by a whisker. As he stepped away for fear of becoming skewered like a kebab, the tree shuddered to the tips of its highest leaves, and then rumbled quietly to a halt. Soon it was just Granny Dazzle's ordinary shady tree again.

Still staring, Jack kicked the piece of bark at his feet back towards the trunk. Suddenly a root struck out from the base of the tree, curled itself around the chunk and whisked it back beneath the grass. If he hadn't seen such amazing things before, Jack would not have believed his eyes.

Sly old Granny Dazzle. All that time they'd imagined she was just sewing or crocheting socks or whatever, while in reality she'd been resting in the tree's embrace, chatting to sister goddesses in the tree bark. He leaned against it now, catching his breath, and at once a vision of Diselda the Dancing Darling filled his mind, just as she was in the portrait in the gallery: young and beautiful beside her vibrant, daring new husband, Lord Jay Bootle-Cadogan. It felt to Jack as though they were both staring at him, beseeching him, begging him to step in and help.

Shaking his head, Jack sighed. Now he had to get on with it. Everyone said it, including a talking tree and a boy a century old, so he supposed he had no choice now. Jack was going to have to sort it all out.

It was time. Time to go back to where it began and get rid of the curse.

Oh, and follow a weird rhyme. Of course.

Establishing where it had all begun was not that easy, as it turned out.

For a start, Albie's memories of what had happened when Jay, Diselda and he had been taking Luxor by storm were all very hazy, blown apart by the explosion Seth had created, and by the devastation of Abydos when Osiris had been interrupted in his regeneration from the Fountain of Youth.

Albie squinted at the boy, whom he'd introduced as Adjo. They were utterly delighted to see each other again, and couldn't stop swapping stories even if Albie couldn't remember them very well.

'Adjo helped with the dig from the start, didn't you, Adj? He came to save me when I'd been ordered to ... what was it? ... oh, hide Osiris' coffin at Abydos. It leapt about like an Afghan hound with me on top of it; do you remember? And then everything went a bit wrong. That was when Jay sent me ... decided to give up the search and marry Diselda instead.'

Everyone looked at each other uncomfortably, not wanting to make Albie relive something that was obviously quite difficult for him.

'Do you remember more than that, Adjo?' asked Jack.

He shrugged. 'Not really, Master Jack. I see Master Cornthwaite shooting up on the top of a leafy elevator into the fountains, and I strike out across the waters to save him because I do not realise that what is happening is good, and then suddenly ZOOMPH! It vanish. I wake up with my nose pressed into black, sparkly sand and Abydos is gone. Everything, PUMPFT! Gone.'

'That was the end of it all,' muttered Albie, his voice scratched and hoarse.

'What about before that?' said Jack, trying to get him back on track. 'What about when Diselda and Jay met?'

'Why don't you ask them yourself?' said Albie bleakly.

Actually, that was a good idea, and Jack could certainly have a chat with his dead rellies. But their own memories of what had gone on seemed a little haphazard too – and in any case, they had not all been together the whole time. Trying to find out from each of them what might or might not have happened was like trying to piece together a jigsaw with several of the pieces missing: all the corners, for instance, and the edges where he'd normally make a start.

What they had so far was Albie's vague recollections of finding Osiris' coffin and of Jay dead and alive; Granny D's famous tales of Jay the great adventurer, and the family legends (from both Bootle-Cadogan and Cornthwaite families) about Jay cheating at poker and being murdered by his opponents by way of a scorpion sting.

Oh, and a pile of Egyptian mythology about Seth and Osiris and a bunch of other gods, which filled the musty library at Lowmount and which Jack didn't have the energy to uncover.

The team, as Jack had started to think of them, blinked despondently at each other, depressed about the prospects of working out yet another riddle, spirits flattened by the tedious drizzle that had started to fall outside.

'Come on,' said Albie suddenly. 'Apart from me – and you, Adjo - this whole room is filled with gods. Surely we can do better than this.'

'Yes, but I'm only a god some of the time,' said Jack. 'Ozzy and Ice aren't up to full strength because of the hole in his head, and Minty ...'

He looked at her. Actually, what about Minty? She was a goddess, after all. She'd just turned up in the same school as Jack, revealed herself at the same time as Seth, and generally hung around since.

'Minty,' he said slowly, not a little worried about how she might react, 'what ... why *are* you here?'

'We're sorting out Ma'at, dufus, remember?' she snorted.

But all at once, the others were staring at Minty in much the same way as Jack.

'That's true, actually, dearest Amentet,' said Albie. 'You told me you were meant to greet me as a dead person after Seth's attack in Luxor, so you were looking out for us then. You're meant to welcome the dead and yet you don't leave us often to undertake your duties in the Field of Rushes. You ... you're always here, and in fact you have been here from when Jack started at Clearwell Comprehensive School.'

Minty squirmed uncomfortably.

As one, Ozzy and Ice turned their regal heads towards the girl and her hawk friend. 'True this is, Amentet,' said Ozzy. 'We are grateful for your assistance, of course, but you were here even before we were summoned by the death of Diselda.'

'Here you were, Amentet,' confirmed Ice, a frown forming a V shape between her frosty blue eyes. 'How is it so?'

'It's no biggy.' With a self-consciousness Jack had never before witnessed, Minty pulled a section of shiny black hair into the corner of her mouth and chewed it furiously. Then she spat it out again. 'It's just ...'

'Just what?' said Jack. Should he be worried about Minty, other than the usual concern about her flooring him in basketball and sucker-punching his kidneys? She had always been at the school, had always hated him – and yet there she was, looking out for him. 'Why are you always around? It can't just be coincidence.'

With a shrug, Minty stared at the floor. 'It's nothing bad.'

'Are you in league, Amentet?' whispered Ice. 'In league with the murderer of Osiris?'

'Of course I'm not!' Now all eyes were on Minty as she scowled back at them, obviously hiding something but still enraged at the suggestion she might be in cahoots with Seth. 'How could you even think that? Would I have spent all these years watching over Dog-boy over there when I could have just delivered him to Seth?'

Albie nodded. 'That's true. She has protected you, Dog-boy. I mean, Jack.'

'Then what is it?' Jack bounded up onto Granny Dazzle's sarcophagus and stared down at Minty's shiny hair. 'Why did you become my protector?'

'Because I promised, okay?' yelled Minty. 'I promised … someone. That I'd look out for you.' She glanced anxiously at Ice. 'Your sister.'

Ozzy, Ice, Adjo and Albie all gasped at this momentous news – rather annoyingly for Jack, as he had not the faintest clue who Ice's sister was. 'Nephthys!' breathed Albie reverently.

'Is that the face in the tree?' Jack said. 'Because that would make sense of why she was talking about sisters and so on.'

'You have seen her!' Ice nodded. 'She is my beloved sister. She will help us restore Osiris to Abydos.'

'And so will you, Jack,' said Albie, 'if the mythology is correct.'

Minty folded her arms smugly. 'And that,' she said, 'is why I had to protect you, even before you knew who you were. I just had to hang around from the moment Diselda turned a century old to be sure of being here when the curse descended.'

Wow. Actually that was … kind of amazing of her. 'You put up with three years of Clearwell Comp for me, before the curse even revived?'

'Yes, Rover.' Minty curled her lip at him, but for the first time Jack could see that the nastiness – or at least some of it – was an act. 'I put up with Guisely's bad breath, and your useless basketball skills, and Fraser asking me out every two weeks for years even though I kept saying no, all to look after a great big fluffy puppy.'

'I don't know what to … hang on; Fraser asked you out?'

Albie and Minty rolled their eyes at the same moment. 'Yeah, *that's* the bit to zoom in on right now,' said Minty. Albie just sucked his teeth disparagingly.

'When?' said Osiris, his voice clear and firm in the muggy atmosphere of the crypt. 'When did Nephthys appoint you?'

'When *they* arrived in Egypt and it was clear that order was about to be disrupted.'

Minty didn't need to say who "they" were. Albie's flushed face announced it, loud and clear: it was when Lord Jay Bootle-Cadogan and his young assistant, Albert Cornthwaite, turned up in search of the resting place of the green god; when a young dancer fell in love and gave Lord Jay her heart on a string.

And suddenly Jack knew what the answer was. The undoing. It had to start now.

'Minty, it's raining outside.'

'Err, I'd noticed,' she growled.

Jack stood and opened the door to the crypt. Soft raindrops swept in across the threshold, momentarily reverting Albie back to Bone as a droplet brushed against his skin. 'Can you make it rain more? Like, loads?'

'Loads?' Minty unfurled herself from the crypt steps and settled the hawk onto his skull cap. 'Yes. I can do loads. But only once.' She looked hard at Jack, obviously working out what he was driving at. If she could turn back time for many minutes with an averagely boring rainstorm, then who knew what would be possible if she delivered a mighty deluge. 'But I might not be able to get you back, Jack. Or Albie.'

Albie jumped up. 'I don't care. I should never have come back anyway. All these years, cursed and ancient, without a family ... If we don't come back, it won't bother me. What ... what about you, Jack?'

It was a risk, for sure.

'Ozzy and Ice, Ice and Ozzy,' said Jack, turning to his friends, 'just how bad will it be if we don't restore order and stuff?'

'Horrific,' said Osiris.

'Unending chaos,' Isis agreed.

Albie pointed to Adjo, whose face was already a little more angular, despite his constant dizzying smile. 'Ozzy's Fountain of Youth is no longer working, so something's going seriously wrong.'

'Endless night, never-ending darkness,' Ozzy reminded them.

Isis nodded. 'And if my sister, goddess of darkness, says it is time, then time it is. She knows it is coming. Coming it is.'

'Endless night?' Jack blinked. 'Well, that we don't need. Just ... just let me go and say ... you know. Just in case.'

The others bowed their heads silently, Albie's eyes melting with sympathy. Even Minty managed to look a tiny bit emotional on his behalf. 'Minty, don't you want to say goodbye to your parents?' he said.

Minty laughed, though not unkindly. 'I'm about five thousand years old, Jack. I live by myself.'

'Oh. Right.' Of course, he'd never checked. Just assumed.

He was on his own, then. It was hard to be selfish about it, when every single one of the others had been living out of their own time for years – decades, even centuries – but it didn't make it any easier to go and bid his parents farewell, knowing he might never come back.

The conversation he overheard when he zipped to his bedroom to fill a back-pack with a few essentials didn't improve matters, either. He could hear his mother being kinder than she'd ever been in the whole of Jack's life, apart from to Roger the dog. Ah. Now that he thought about it, it was Roger the dog she was talking to. Recently he'd been sleeping longer and longer and refusing to go to walks, and now Jack's super-hearing told him that his mother was in the boot room where Roger's disgustingly smelly bed resided.

'Come on, old boy. Just have a little drink for me. Just a tiny bit. That's it. Good. You'll be better soon, really you will.'

There was a short silence and then, to his horror, Jack's mother began to cry. 'Don't die on me. Don't you die on me, do you hear? I won't be able to bear it without you. You're a cantankerous old so and so, but I still adore you, you silly thing.'

Then she was out-and-out sobbing. Jack hovered beyond the doorway, not sure whether to step in and comfort her. She'd probably be completely embarrassed to be found crying in a cupboard. And how much better was he going to make it when he made his statement? 'Just come to say goodbye, Mother – got to go far, far away and maybe never come back.' Then, just to put the icing on the top: 'Oh, and Bone's coming with me and you may never see him again either. See ya.'

He leaned his head against the door and took a deep breath, ready to plunge in ... but at the last second he changed his mind. He couldn't bother her now. There was every chance he'd make it back and then he'd have upset her for nothing. Instead, he zipped to his father's room, watched him sleep for a second or two, then left a note on the kitchen table.

BASKETBALL COMPETITION IN GLASGOW. AWAY A FEW DAYS. DON'T WORRY ABOUT ME - BONE'S COMING TOO. TAKE CARE, LOVE JACK xxxxxxxxxx

He left ten kisses, which was nine more than he'd usually add even if he was feeling mushy. Then he grabbed his bag, pictured the crypt, and zipped off to meet the team.

'Ready?' said Albie.

Was he? Jack had done some curious and difficult things of late, but this was about the strangest and the most difficult. Still, if he did manage to remove the curse – and get back to the present – perhaps it would make everything better in this world too. And if he didn't, there wouldn't be much world to worry about ...

'Ready,' he said.

They all stepped out into the drizzle-glazed graveyard where the jackals circled warily. Around Vera Cornthwaite's gravestone, they all linked hands. The rain quickly became a downpour as Minty squeezed her eyes together tightly.

'It's not enough,' she said gruffly after a minute or two, opening one eye. 'I'll have to draft in the big guns. Ice?'

Ice nodded quickly, raising her right arm and Minty's left. 'Nephthys, goddess of darkness and sister of storms, we call on you,' she cried, the words whipping eerily around the headstones. 'Sister, assist us now! Help Amentet in the name of Osiris, and in the name of Anubis, your son!'

'Your ... your what?' shrieked Jack, but the question was snatched away by the hurricane now battering them from all sides, whisking the baying jackals away across the hedges like Toto across the rainbow. Hailstones the size of tennis balls cracked against the granite gravestones with the sound of pistol-shots, and an awful, supernatural groaning emanated from Granny Dazzle's tree as it creaked and bent and eventually began to snap under the assault of the blasts of wind.

Jack cried out. 'Careful! That tree's precious!' But the tree itself screeched as a goddess spirit rose from its uppermost branches, coiling against the blackened skies.

Even more horrifying were the sobs and thrashing motions of his friend, Bone, reliving some horrendous past event volubly and agonisingly. He tried to cover his ears, but his hands burned as he lifted them. Grains of sand ground into Jack's face, scouring away his stubble, his skin, the flesh from his bones ...

'Stop it, Minty!' he screamed. 'This is unbearable! It's not a bit like –'

It stopped abruptly, all at once, to be replaced by a breathless, weighty silence.

'... the other times.'

Jack lifted his head. No wonder he'd felt as though his face were being rubbed with sandpaper. He was lying face-first on a beach.

He looked up again.

No. Not a beach.

The desert.

The sun beat down on the back of his head. Jack reached a hand out gingerly. Curly hair – it was his own head, not the dog-headed presence of Anubis.

So he was stranded somewhere in the desert, just a normal teenage boy.

And actually, it was a bit worse than that. He glanced around, quickly confirming his earlier suspicion when he noticed that silence had descended.

The others had all disappeared.

He was completely – completely - on his own.

But not for long, it would seem. Along the horizon, a number of figures were silhouetted against the rising sun. Marching figures.

Marching, Jack guessed, towards him.

Chapter 4

Jack sat up on the sand, his head aching miserably and his skin prickling with the slightly scorched sensation that he sometimes got from playing tennis in the midday sun. The figures were definitely getting closer – or was it further away? It was hard to tell as he squinted into the blinding sunlight. He didn't know, either, whether to *hope* that they were going away or heading towards him. It might be Albie and the others, in which case he would be very glad to see them, or it might be a bunch of Seth supporters, in which case he'd be happier burying into the sand like a snake and trying to disappear.

There was clearly no place to hide other than beneath the sand dunes, though, and the shapes were increasing in size so they had obviously seen him.

'Up you get, you idiot,' Jack told himself, in a voice that sounded uncannily and rather shockingly like his own father's. It was certainly a Dad-like thing to say – seemingly gruff and uncaring, but actually preparing him to be on his feet, standing as an equal to whoever or whatever should loom over him.

He struggled to a standing position, slightly whoozy from the transportation that Minty had provided, and shook the grains of sand from his hair, his hoodie, the pockets of his jeans. It had got everywhere; he felt as if he'd lost an entire layer of skin. It was his human skin, he noticed, and that was probably a good thing. Most people were alarmed when a large boy with a jackal's head popped up in front of them.

These figures, however, were not most people.

What they were was ... well, they were mutants. Rather like Jack in Doghead form, they were partly one thing, and partly another. At the front of the platoon – for that was evidently what it was – strode three enormous men wearing skirts of looped, bleached cotton topped by broad leather belts. The broad leather belts led up to broad leathery chests, and on to broad, muscly shoulders and then up to a feathered neck and the head of some kind of bird of prey. A hungry one, Jack would have guessed if forced.

The women, however, were even more extraordinary. There were seven of them in two rows behind the bird-headed men, so the platoon fanned out in a bell shape with four of the women ... things ... at the back. Jack could understand perfectly why you'd want these women bringing up the rear. This time the mutation was reversed: each woman had a human face, hair and neck, all beautifully made up with deep kohl-lined eyes with precise little flicks at the corners that would have made Granny Dazzle weep with envy, and long tresses that flowed over their shoulders in curls or waves and even plaits. Beneath the hair, it was a horror story – a potentially fatal, terrifying horror story. Each of the women had human shoulders and arms that melded seamlessly with the body of a scorpion. The gleaming casing around their lower halves looked as impenetrable as black marble, and Jack doubted anyway whether anyone would get close enough to attack their legs – all eight of them – as a venomous sac the size of a football pulsed malignantly on the end of each curved tail, dangling directly over the scorpion woman's back but ready to lash outwards and spear an enemy in seconds.

Jack really hoped he wasn't an enemy, but all the signs pointed to these people-things being in Seth's employ. They were upon him now, stamping to a halt in their three-rowed formation.

Here goes, thought Jack.

'Hello!' he cried optimistically, holding up a hand in greeting.

The first bird-headed man opened its beak. Jack was expecting a croak or a caw of some kind, but instead a human voice appeared from between the mandibles. 'I emulate your tongue.'

He didn't show his tongue, weirdly; instead he nodded, snapped his beak shut and stared at Jack with sparkling black eyes.

'Oh! Tongue! Like … my language. Yes, English,' Jack confirmed, doing his best not to raise his voice and shout slowly like his father did with "foreigners". 'Thank you.'

The hawk-man nodded more deeply, then cried: 'By Re and in the name of the great Pharaoh, declare yourself!'

'I … I'm Jack Bootle-Cadogan, from Lowmount in England,' he started, but then he ground to a halt. What was he supposed to say? I've come to restore Ma'at? Take me to your leader?

Actually, he realised, that might work.

'And I am here to talk to your leader. About ... Ma'at.'

The scorpion tales suddenly bristled like a row of deadly scimitars, all pointing relentlessly at some tiny exposed piece of his flesh as the hawk-men turned their broad shiny chests towards him.

'What know you of Ma'at, Jack of the Golden Hair?' snapped the second man, looking him up and down dubiously.

Jack's hand flew up to his head. Golden hair? What was he talking about?

'That's probably just sand,' he said with a grin. 'And about Ma'at? Well, I know it's the natural order of things, and I need to talk to ...' What had they called him? '... the great Pharaoh! Please,' he added politely.

The strange collection of mutant people paused for a second, staring at each other. Suddenly, to Jack's astonishment, they all burst into raucous laughter. Then the women spoke as one but all at different notes, so it sounded like a chord played on the harpsichord that Granny Dazzle had kept in her rooms.

'The Great Pharaoh IS the natural order, Jack of the Golden Hair. He is Ma'at!'

'Pharaoh is not in need of your assistance, golden one,' scoffed the third bird man.

Wow. They were all a little obsessed with this golden thing, thought Jack. They were going to be very disappointed when he'd had a shower and rinsed it all off. They were also very, very proud of their king, and given what Jack knew about Tutankhamun and other pharaohs (mostly from his shockingly brief visit to the British Museum) he could guess that they wouldn't welcome much advice from outsiders. He'd have to make this much more urgent, somehow.

Wishing he had Albie with him so they could take a stab at which pharaoh was on the throne, Jack nodded carefully.

'I'm sure he's a very great leader, your pharaoh, but I need to tell him that …' There was nothing else for it. He'd have to just tell them the truth and hope it was enough to win him an audience. And not get him killed. 'Your god Osiris is in trouble. And if I don't help him, the natural order will be destroyed. In your world and in mine. Total chaos, never-ending darkness, that kind of disaster.'

To his alarm, the group seemed to act instinctively to this news, sweeping around Jack in a tightly knit circle, every staff and poison sac aimed directly at him. 'Who tells you this, stranger?'

Hmm. So much for Golden Jack and all that. 'Well, quite a few people. Gods, in fact. Amentet, for instance, and … um … Nephthys.'

A volley of gasps rattled around the circle. 'Nephthys speaks with you? How?' cried the conjoined voices of the scorpion women.

'From her ... she was a tree.' Jack shrugged. It sounded weird, but then he was surrounded by some very odd creatures, so perhaps it wouldn't seem so unusual to them.

Two of the men thought about it for a second, then nodded, and the first one to address Jack lowered his staff towards Jack's midriff. 'Is it you who endangers Osiris, Jack of the Golden Hair? Speak truthfully, or die!'

'No,' said Jack quickly, although he didn't see how that was going to stop him from being attacked. It sounded like one of those awful unanswerable questions – say no and they won't believe you, so they'll stab you through the heart with a pointy stick or a poisonous barb, but say yes, and they'll do it anyway. 'I promise that I am not the one who endangers Osiris. It's—' He'd been about to say 'Seth', but then thought better of it. He still didn't know whether this was Seth's mutant army, as he wasn't able to get any information out of them. They were the ones asking all the questions. Impossible questions.

'I'm his friend,' he said simply. 'Honestly!'

Ten pairs of beady eyes swept across the circle, looking for assent from each other, as Jack sweated in the centre and tried to shake sand out of his trousers without anyone noticing. He had the distinct feeling they were communicating silently, because suddenly one of the women, with slightly coppery hair and paler skin, bent over and sniffed at him. Then she shook her head and the whole group seemed to relax.

'By the wisdom of Thoth,' said the first hawk-man, 'we shall find out if you speak true.'

'How?' squeaked Jack, rather dreading the answer.

'We take you to him. To Pharaoh.'

And with Jack in the centre like the pupil of a terrible eye - with scorpion stings for eyelashes - they turned together and crunched their way across the sand, back towards the distant horizon that was now blazed unforgivingly beneath a tangerine sun.

They seemed to walk for hours, and Jack sincerely wished that he'd had the forethought to turn into his Anubis form when the creature-people had first approached. Maybe they'd have accepted him straight away if he was enormous and in two sections, like they were.

Or maybe ... maybe that would have just antagonised them. They seemed to find him quite amusing as an English and apparently golden boy, and at least this way he'd got what he wanted: to be taken to the Pharaoh's palace. He guessed that if the others had landed nearby, they would also be under guard somewhere at the court. If he heard they were trapped there he could do some sneaky transforming and bust them all out. After he'd had a chance to meet the pharaoh and try to warn him about the threat to poor Ozzy and general Ma'at, of course ...

He trudged across the desert, feeling like a kid in the back of a car being driven somewhere mysterious and far, far away.

'Are we there yet?' he asked, suddenly aware that they hadn't passed any pyramids or sphinxes or temples, or anything that he would have imagined would be close to Pharaoh's palace.

The hawk-man laughed. 'Is Little Gold fatigued?'

'Yes,' replied Jack, 'although I'm really not golden.'

'Fear not,' said the man, ignoring him. 'You will see the palace when we reach the crest.'

Crest. Great. Uphill in a desert. A strangely empty desert that was not crowded with all the ancient buildings that Albie would have loved to see. Where, for instance, were the famous pyramids? Nowhere in eyeshot, that was for sure.

A bead of sweat trickled into his eye. Wishing he'd thought of it before, Jack stripped off his hoodie and wrapped it around his head. It was cooler all round, ironically – which was a good thing when the heat haze above the sand dune made the air look alive, a squirming, breathing, undulating transparent beast. He was losing his marbles. He probably had heat-stroke. He'd suffer death by sweating if they didn't get there soon.

But suddenly there it was – a palace indeed; a long, low building the size of Lowmount, built all on one level and all in sparkling white. On either side of a vast latticed doorway, at least three times the height of Jack's own impressive oak doors at home, stood a pair of statues of people Jack knew and loved. Ozzy, sporting a long and pointy beard and a white headdress, was painted a bright, lively green, with the crook and flail folded across his chest. On the other side of the doorway, Ice stared out across the desert, enormous cow horns sprouting from her head. Between the horns, a disk as bright as the sun that had beaten down on Jack's head for hours was glowing with a strange beauty, and Ice's pale blue dress seemed to waft in the heat.

'Ah! There they are,' said Jack, genuinely touched to see his little buddies being so revered. And not quite so little. 'My friends. Very impressive. Well done.'

The nearest scorpion female shoved him in the back. 'The great leaders will decide,' she growled ominously.

'Sure.' Jack stumbled on towards the palace entrance. 'Where are the pyramids? I thought there'd be pyramids.'

'Pyramids,' parroted the second soldier. 'I know not what they are.'

'You know: four sides, triangular, pointy top.'

The hawkish man shook his feathered head and showed Jack the end of his staff. 'Pointy top,' he muttered. His meaning was very clear. Keep talking, and this will be stuffed in your eye before you even see it coming.

So there was nothing for it to but to move forward steadily, keeping time with the regular tread of the birdmen and the scuffling tap-tap of fifty six scorpion feet, slithering between them down the steep top of the sand dune that protected the palace from the elements and any infiltrators who might dare to trek across the desert.

Finally, Jack found himself on a wide avenue leading directly to the palace doors. It was lined with trees and the occasional stall selling fruit, and throngs of normal people who obviously saw him as the curiosity - despite the fact that all the men, women and children seemed to be dressed in skirts, dresses or nothing at all with not a shred of embarrassment, and the creatures leading Jack into the pharaoh's home were only part-human.

He stepped beneath the massive archway, nodding upwards. Sure, they were only statues, and he didn't want to say anything for fear of being pronged, but he wanted Ozzy and Ice to know that he was on it. Here he was, about to meet the current pharaoh, and somehow to convince him that Ozzy needed his help and possibly his protection. A chill ran down his spine with this thought. No doubt many battles had been fought in the protection of Ozzy, and for the first time, Jack realised that his mission might just start a war.

Passing tinkling fountains and groups of palace courtiers in white, silky versions of what the street-sellers outside had been wearing, he held his breath. Perhaps he hadn't thought this through enough. What was he going to say to the pharaoh? How should he even greet a pharaoh? Your majesty? Your highness? Your pharaohness?

He'd have to work it out imminently as the inner courtroom doors were ahead of them, inlaid with gold and faience so they glimmered and blinked in the dappled sunlight. A soldier stepped to either side and shoved the massive doors apart, and Jack was led into the vast cathedral of a room by the first hawk-man and a circlet of scuttling scorpi-women.

'Jack of the Golden Hair seeks an audience with you, Great Pharaoh.'

Ah. Great Pharaoh. That was what he should say.

There was a long pause, then a fluid voice said, 'So speak, Jack of the Golden Hair.'

Then he was hauled forward in front of the king, and he realised that he didn't have to say anything formal at all – because ahead of him, on two majestic thrones which he'd seen replicated in the ante-room before the Field of Rushes, sat his two friends.

'Ozzy! It's you!' Jack laughed with delight and a fair helping of relief. 'Ice 'n' Ozzy, Ozzy 'n' Ice! I didn't know you were a pharaoh too, Oz.'

Two pairs of eyes widened slightly as Jack took in their appearance. It was much as the statues at the door had depicted: both grown up, both very regal, and Ozzy the proud owner of a new beard.

'This is going to make it so much easier! Clever Minty,' cried Jack, but just as he stepped forward to clasp their hands, the birdman thrust him onto the floor.

'He says he is your friend, Great Osiris.'

Great Osiris stared down at Jack as if he was a bug on the rug.

'Friend? Do you know this boy, my queen?'

Ice shook her head gently. 'Know him I do not. And you?'

'Ice, it's me! Jack BC! Look, I knew you were going to say that: know him I do not. That's just how you always respond to Ozzy.'

'Shush, now,' ordered the great pharaoh. 'Wepsit, my proud avian defender, I have never before seen this golden-haired stranger. We must ensure our safety first before we speak with him.'

'You are wise, brother,' said a dark, insidious voice.

It was only then that Jack noticed the pair of thrones set back behind the pharaoh's. On one sat a beautiful woman, stroking the falcon on her lap. She cast her eyes swiftly in Jack's direction then lowered them again to the bird's head, but it was enough for Jack to catch a warning in them. Take care. Look about.

The dark voice continued. 'Wepsit,' the man said to the leader of the birdmen, 'I suggest we silence him.'

'My lord Set,' said Wepsit, bowing his head.

And just as Jack stared at the man seated behind Ozzy's shoulder, taking in the name, taking in the pig-like, cruel face, Wepsit gestured to one of the women. She raised her tail and struck Jack on the bicep. Unable to save himself, Jack cried out as the venom seared through his arm, pumping towards his heart, and suddenly he toppled forward, blanking out the pain, the horror, the concerned frowns of Big Ozzy and Ice, and the smirking, porcine features of their mutual enemy. Seth.

Chapter 5

'For crying out loud, Albert,' bawled a familiar voice. 'I've done my utmost to drag you out of the gutter of life, but if you will insist on grovelling in the dirt there's very little more to be done about it. No, sir; he's with me. Yes, and the boy too; I hired him yesterday. No, I don't want .... Away with you!'

'J – Jack?' whispered Albie uncertainly.

Jack had never called him Albert, it was true – but someone else had, many years ago. And Jack had never taken that imperious tone with him, though many others had, not so many years ago.

Cautiously prising open one eye, Albie found he was peering through a shattered lens that obscured his vision of whoever was ranging around above him, hauling Adjo to his feet and dusting him down to an accompaniment of colourful curses.

'And now he's calling me Jack, Adjo. What the devil happened to the pair of you? Help me get him up, will you?'

A face loomed into view, jagged like a kaleidoscope, and Albie's heart nearly failed him.

It was Jay. Lord Jay Bootle-Cadogan, his mentor and benefactor, larger than life as he had always been, until he'd had no life in him at all. As a meaty first curled around his collar and hoisted him into the air, Albie looked around him for clues: there was Adjo, still a little older than when Jay had last seen him, but he wouldn't be the type to notice such nuanced transformations; around them was the souk, a riot of colour and aroma that assaulted every sense, and just behind the be-suited body that was brushing detritus from his suit was a very familiar sight indeed – the Oasis Orchid.

Jay propped Albie up on both feet and shook him heartily by the shoulders. 'Do I have to slap your face like a hysterical woman, Cornthwaite? Snap out of it or you'll force me to do something I won't enjoy one bit. Well, all right, perhaps just a little bit—'

'Bootle-Cadogan!' cried Albie, interrupting his lord and master in his tirade. 'Jay! It truly is you.'

Before the man had a moment to respond, Albie hurled himself forward and flung both arms around him, squeezing him as if his very life depended on it. Perhaps it did, no less, because it had all started here, with Jay in Luxor – alive! Alive and well enough to be rude and demanding and effortlessly charming when the mood suited him.

He didn't look particularly charming at the present moment, however.

'Get ... get off me, man!' barked Jay, half-laughing but clearly embarrassed about the very public display of affection. Suddenly Albie remembered that this was a different era - a time when men shook hands formally instead of fist-bumping and slapping each other's shoulders in a semi-hug; when men never cried as Albie was beginning to now; when it was the norm to be strong and upright and reserved, not snivelling and gushing with exuberance and emotion …

With a start, Albie let go of Jay and straightened his broken spectacles. 'Forgive me,' he stammered, watching Jay's bewildered expression change from anger to laughter, then to sheer puzzlement and back to laughter again. He always was as capricious as the desert wind.

Jay clapped a hand on his shoulder and stared seriously into his face. 'Are you quite well, old chap? Did you receive a blow to the head? I only sent you out to the souk to find some more trowels for the dig, but then I heard this tremendous uproar about … sand storms or some such nonsense, and here you both are in the middle of it. Should I send for the doctor?'

'No, no, I'm quite well, thank you, Jay.' Albie was so very well, in fact, that he could have hugged himself for joy, let alone Jay. 'Quite, quite, quite …' Careful. That was far too many "quites" for 1922. 'I'm fine. No need for medical assistance.'

'Good! Because in truth, I wouldn't know where to find him anyway.' Jay smacked him on the arm. 'Bit of a curmudgeon, I've been told. Rather down in the dumps after seeing to all those poor boys in the war.'

Jay himself had sailed through the First World War without so much as a scratch, being one of the handful of pilots who could fly a twin-prop with one hand and wave with the other, and more in demand at country shows than in dog fights. He'd had one or two skirmishes, though, and had won each of them with barely a mark to his plane or his burnished and handsome face.

Actually Albie remembered the doctor – from another time. Some time in the future from where they were standing right now, or at least that was what he was guessing. If they were still looking for supplies, still great friends, and only just hiring Adjo, then the new dig was just ahead of them.

He calculated quickly. They were in Luxor, so they'd moved from Giza about a week ago after digging there had led nowhere. He was following a lead about the resting place of Osiris. He hadn't yet destroyed Abydos and the Fountain of Youth, so that meant it was probably mid-May, just about the time when they opened up the tomb … and Jay met someone special.

'Diselda,' whispered Albie, unable to prevent himself.

'Where? Can you see her?' Jay whispered back, ducking under a canopy. 'I want to get my hair oiled before we meet again tonight – and grab a bath, now that I'm covered in dust.'

'No,' said Albie. 'No, no. Ohhhh no. No, no, no, no, no.'

Good Lord, after so many years of not being able to speak, his mouth was running away with itself like a Stephenson engine.

Jay shook his head, mystified. 'So why did you say her name?'

'I ... didn't. See her, I mean. I thought I did, but I didn't. It was someone else.'

'Right.' Jay raised his eyebrows at Adjo, who had been observing the whole exchange with increasingly round eyes. 'Are you similarly addled?'

'Addled, Lord Jay?'

Jay tapped his temple. 'Mad. Lost your marbles.'

'Ahhh, Lord Jay.' Adjo released his mighty torrent of laughter. 'I am having no marbles at all.'

'He's fine, too, Jay,' said Albie quickly. He had to pull his act together, and Adjo's too. 'In fact, Adjo – shouldn't you let your family know that the sand storm didn't destroy you?' He winked slowly behind his fractured lens, then stopped. The effect of a hundred eyes closing at glacial speed was probably quite nauseating. 'I believe your father and at least two siblings are currently selling their wares on the slipper stall.'

'That is true, Master Cornthwaite,' said Adjo. His hushed tone spiralled up like a tornado as he figured out that he was about to see his family again, at the age they'd been when they all first met. 'That is very, very true! Ah! I shall see my father and my mother, and my ... my grandmother too, and all my four sisters and two brothers, all young and alive! Alive!'

'Indeed you shall,' said Albie with a smile.

Jay huffed out an enormous sigh as Adjo raced away, with his soles kicking up dust beneath his long white robe and his hands above his head, waving joyfully at everyone he passed.

'Was it the tea?' he asked eventually. 'I've warned you about the natives' tea, Albert. It can contain some very peculiar ingredients.'

'You can't call them natives, Jay,' hissed Albie.

'Why not?'

'It's not proper.'

'Well, what am I meant to call them?'

'Just …' It was the old arguments again – the same discussion Albie had to have as Bone with Jack's father, and the one he'd had over and over with Jay. Servant. Slave. Native. They were all terrible words which could no longer be countenanced – but countenance them they still did in the early twentieth century. 'Call them locals,' he finished flatly.

Jay shrugged. 'Fine! So don't drink the locals' tea. You're too young and skinny for it anyway. And don't even think about having a drink at the Oasis Orchid. Much too strong for the likes of you, ye young whipper-snapper.'

It was a mixed blessing, being back, thought Albie with a sigh. On the one hand, he was delighted to be back with his old, old friend and employer, in this magnificent place where history and archaeology (and pharaohs) were king. On the other, Albie had lived through another century – a century of deprivation and atrocities and massive,

massive advances – and it was going to be hard accepting some of the things that Lord Jay Bootle-Cadogan said or did without thought.

He was stopped in his musing by a voice calling out to him. 'Albie. Bone! Albert Cornthwaite!'

'Sounds like you've upset someone else, Corny,' said Jay with a grin. 'Oh, and it's a girl! Nicely done, old chap. Nicely done.'

'Minty!' Albie cried. For some reason, he had assumed she'd disappeared with Jack, as his friend was nowhere to be seen. 'Where's Jack?'

The girl stomped up to him, rolling her eyes. 'I don't know. Off on his own little adventure, I expect. You know what Jack's like.'

'Aha! So who is the inimitable Jack?' said Jay, an expression of great amusement contorting his moustachioed lips. 'And who, my dear lady, might you be?'

Minty took one look at Jay's face and turned scarlet, obviously realising that she might have scuppered their plans by blurting out all of Albie's names at once. 'Minty West,' she said abruptly, not bothering to explain who Jack was, as she stuck out a grimy hand.

Jay kissed it. Naturally. 'Delighted, I'm sure. Now tell me, what has my dear Albert been doing to incur your wrath?'

'Nothing! Nothing at all.' Minty tried to smile amiably, and it was only then that Albie realised how little she did it. It was more like she was baring her teeth, and even Jay backed away a little. 'I just haven't seen him for a while and thought I'd say hello. Um. Hello.'

'Yes, hello.' Albie steered her to the edge of the souk. 'Actually, Miss West, we all just had a little shake-up in the dust storm and we're going to sit in the shade and drink some tea. Coffee. Would you care for some?'

Minty glared at him as if he'd just offered her arsenic. 'Thank you, but no,' she snapped. 'I just wanted to check … to say hello, and now that I've … said hello, there's something I need to do.'

'Join us later, perhaps, for a gin sling at the Oasis Orchid,' cried Jay chirpily.

'Thank you, but no,' she repeated like a parrot, clearly quite pleased with her sudden grasp of 1920s etiquette. 'I'm only fifteen in your years.'

'Oh! Apologies, my dear. You look so mature.'

'Well, that's because I am,' snapped Minty. 'Looks,' she continued with a deep scowl in Albie's direction, 'can be very, very deceiving.'

She nodded curtly to them both, one after the other, and then strode away through the market, ploughing a furrow through the crowd with her confident stride and unforgiving brow, effortlessly and rather magnificently intimidating to all around. Albie almost laughed, though whether it was at Jay being so discomfited or Minty failing to mention that she was actually fifteen plus infinity, he couldn't have said. Instead he scratched the edges of his thin moustache, and nudged his old friend.

'Come to think of it, Jay, I really could do with a drink of some kind, and perhaps something sweet to eat. That storm was quite unsettling.'

Jay looked mortified at his lack of attention. 'Of course, dear chap, of course! Look, sit yourself down on this stool – I'll put it in the shade so it's perhaps half a degree cooler – and I'll go and find you some victuals. A strong coffee and some of that semolina cake; that should do the trick.'

'Basbousa,' said Albie.

'I beg your pardon?'

'The cake. It's called basbousa.'

'Ah! Right. The nati ... the local word for it. Well, all of that coming up in mere minutes. You sit tight, my friend, and I'll be back in two shakes of a camel's tale.'

And, as luck or misfortune would have it, it was in those sparse minutes while Jay was away that he saw her.

Diselda the Dancing Darling was floating out of the back door of the Oasis Orchid with her feathered costume over her arm, threading her way across the souk as gossamer-light as a feather herself. Albie's chest constricted; for a moment he had to lean over, trying to breathe. It was what he'd hoped for and imagined for all those years, although of course he had never dreamed that they could really ever be together despite his ardent – and it truly was ardent – love for Diselda Carruthers. She had given Jay her heart on a string, and it was to Jay that she was always committed.

His eyes followed her through the market. She was almost stepping in Minty's wake, a wisp of linen and pale cotton contrasting with her daringly short hair, bobbed in a fashion that had caused girls to be fired from their jobs in department stores back home in England. Diselda didn't care; not for her the shackles of regular society. There was always – had always been, for the rest of her life – something uniquely sturdy about her. For all the fey fairy costumes, she was pure steely individuality on the inside.

Albie felt sick to his stomach. He hadn't imagined this awful longing would be revived, but here he was, mooning after his friend's beloved across an Egyptian market. He could see her now, in the doorway of a rug vendor's shop, talking to someone out of sight.

Leaning forward, Albie nearly fell off his stool and then realised how ridiculous he was being. He didn't have to stay on the stool. He could just walk right up to her and … say hello, like Minty. They'd met before; it would not be inappropriate. Good lord, man, he admonished himself. You're over a century old! Surely you've worked out how to speak to the woman you love without making an errant fool of yourself?

Spurred on, he stood and walked unsteadily along the alleyway between the stalls. Adjo called out to him from behind a mountain of moccasins; he flipped a hand at him absently and carried on. It was as if he were in a trance, he thought as he neared the rug-seller. Fortunately, Adjo's shout was enough to snap him out of his reverie, because just as he rounded the edges of the bazaar he spotted who it was that Diselda had been speaking with in her usual animated, finger-flying fashion.

He'd half-expected it to be Jay, but instead it was someone else he knew. Minty. She was talking to Diselda earnestly, sternly even, and suddenly she reached into the pocket of her long, high-waisted dress and pulled out an object. Diselda took it from her, looking uncharacteristically nervous, and then she nodded and draped the object around her neck.

It was her locket. The heart on a string. The one that Minty had told her to wear for her protection.

The very same locket that, later that day, Diselda would give to Jay to claim him as her one true love.

Except … except maybe it wasn't too late. She hadn't given it to Jay yet. Perhaps he hadn't yet claimed her heart. Perhaps someone else – a young archaeologist with great prospects as a leading antiquities expert – could steal her heart away.

He didn't want to hurt Jay. Of course he didn't; he admired Jay as a man and as a historian, and couldn't thank him enough for the opportunities he had given him as a local man with a future only as an undertaker in the family business. He had unleashed Albie's greatest passion – or at least the subject which had been his greatest passion until a certain dancing girl had chanced his way. But Jay was charming, rich and accomplished, and would find love with the next pretty face that appeared along his path, whereas Albie could only love one woman. This woman, smiling at Minty, nodding and passing the locket's chain through her delicate fingers.

And so he decided, even though he knew the dangers of meddling with ancient history, that this was his gift. He had been brought back to this moment so that he could right the wrongs of the past.

He arrived at the Oasis Orchid a full hour before he'd arranged to meet Jay, who had eventually caught up with him at the guesthouse, having drunk Albie's coffee and eaten his cake in frustration at being left alone. The evening had barely begun, and most of the girls were still in the bar area, downing some Dutch courage or begging the waiters for fresh lemonade.

Diselda was standing on her own, staring dreamily beyond the stage. Swallowing his nerves, Albie forced himself to march over to her.

'Good evening, Miss Carruthers. How startlingly beautiful you look tonight.'

He almost gagged. The words sounded pathetic and ridiculous pouring out of his mouth. Jay could carry it off, of course, but not Albie.

Diselda, however, didn't look too concerned. 'Mr Cornthwaite!' She peered over his shoulder as if expecting someone else, and then turned the full beam of her lovely eyes onto him. 'It's very nice of you to say so. Are you enjoying Luxor?'

'I am indeed,' he said nervously. 'It holds treasures of which I could never even have dreamed. And talking of treasures,' he added quickly in case he ran out of courage, 'that is a ... a lovely locket you're wearing.'

'Oh, this!' She giggled, running the necklace through her hand. 'I received it today from a mysterious soothsayer in the bazaar. She told me it would keep me safe, but that in order for it to work I must give it to someone extremely special tonight.' Her eyes sparkled at the very thought.

'And ... ah. And do you have a special person in mind?'

Smiling self-consciously, Diselda clutched the locket tight. 'I believe I do. Someone we both know, Mr Cornthwaite.'

Albie nodded, then nodded some more as he tried to convince himself not to do the thing he was about to do. Jay didn't deserve it – he'd done no wrong. But didn't Albie deserve happiness too? And Diselda! If history repeated itself, she would find herself a widow at eighteen, and a pregnant one at that. If she chose Albie instead, she could have a full and happy life, with her husband by her side.

Hardly able to believe his own actions, Albie stopped nodding in case it was beginning to look fatuous, and took Diselda's hand. 'I do know who you mean, of course, Miss Carruthers. And Lord Jay has certainly mentioned that one of the dancing girls has caught his eye. He just ... just didn't tell me which one.'

'There ... there's more than one?'

Beneath his fingers, he felt Diselda's fingers tremble.

'Um, yes, yes,' he said, feeling more treacherous and vile with every passing second. 'There's usually more than one.'

That much was true, usually. But actually, Jay had had eyes only for Diselda since they'd arrived in Luxor. Damn it! He couldn't do this. Cursing himself for the terrible disloyalty he'd perpetrated, Albie dropped Diselda's hand.

'I'm sorry,' he stuttered. 'Jay is a good man, at heart. He truly is. I've said too much, and naturally you must give your necklace to whomsoever you wish.'

She lifted her little chin high. 'Oh, I will, Mr Cornthwaite, you can be sure of it. I most certainly will. To a good man with a strong heart, who I'm sure will love me dearly.'

'Yes,' said Albie sadly, realising that what he'd said had made no difference anyway. 'That is what you must do.'

But three hours later, to the enormous surprise of Lord Jay Bootle-Cadogan and everyone else in the Oasis Orchid, that was exactly what Diselda the Dancing Darling did. Whispering to him, 'Now you have my heart on a string,' the dancer tore her eyes away from Jay and draped her locket over Albie's head.

A good man with a strong heart, who loved her dearly.

He'd ruined it. He'd ruined it entirely. And he couldn't even give the locket back without humiliating Diselda still further. She kissed his cheek and he knew his heart should be soaring, but instead it tolled out an ominous roll like a death knell, or the blessed funeral march.

Unable to look anyone in the eye, Albie waited until Diselda was back on the stage for her final dance and then fled from the bar, away from the hurt and disbelieving eyes of Lord Jay, and the resolute firmness of Diselda, and the utter, terrifying fury of Minty who met him in the doorway, cast a glance at the locket, and then swept away in disgust.

It was just as he'd thought. Of course. He'd ruined absolutely everything.

Chapter 6

Jack came to in a position that, because of his work as Anubis, seemed almost comfortingly familiar to him. He was lying on his back on the top of a huge sarcophagus that would have accommodated the whole Bootle-Cadogan family and their staff. Nope, didn't even like saying that, even though it was only in his head. Their Bones. That was better.

He was stretched out in a large X shape, piniuned at the wrists and ankles by heavy manacles which appeared to be forged from some tempered metal. Steel, perhaps. Jack tried flexing his lower arms, but achieved nothing apart from a loud clanking from the chains around his limbs. Blimey. They weren't taking any chances.

Still nursing a headache and a very sore arm, Jack thanked his dog-god qualities that enabled him to heal so quickly. He was pretty sure that an injection from a poison sac the size of a grapefruit would have killed most people outright, or at least hospitalised them for a few weeks – and he was pretty convinced he hadn't been unconscious for very long. He wasn't even hungry, for a start, and as he was ravenous most of the time this suggested to him that it hadn't been days and days since he last ate. (Unless they'd fed him while he was asleep. Eugh.)

Rotating his head left and right, he tried to get the measure of his surroundings. Sarcophagus – tick. Weird temple like a grown-up version of the Lowmount crypt, with candles in sconces made from a strange amber glass and peculiar paintings on the walls – tick. Ozzy and Ice perched on the ends of a flying carpet made from a camp-bed – well, almost a tick. No camp-bed, and they weren't perched, but they were definitely in the room with him.

They didn't look like his Ozzy and Ice, though. They were tall and regal and filled the room with all sorts of things that Jack suspected he was going to have to cultivate: charisma, and presence, and an air of knowing what they were doing. Ice clearly wasn't about to wail, and Ozzy was just a normal dark skin colour, not some freaky shade of green. Not that freaky would have bothered them, obviously. He'd only had to witness his armed guard to work that one out.

'He awakes,' said Ozzy in his new mature voice, so deep that Jack almost wanted to giggle. It matched the magnificent goatee-type beard, which looked like an ice-cream cone attached to his chin.

'Awakes he does.' Yep. Not that much had changed.

Jack tried sitting up but the chains held him fast. 'Hi!' he said pitifully from his prone position. 'Awake I do. Could I get up, do you think?'

Ozzy eyed him warily for a good minute and a half, and then gestured to one of the guards – Wotsit, or whatever he was called - to unchain him. 'Hold his arms back. I trust him not.'

'So why are you releasing me?'

Osiris smiled at his queen. 'Isis convinced me that it was unseemly to treat our visitors thus. You may be an imposter, or you might indeed have important news for us. My apologies for our earlier intervention.'

'You are restored to health most quickly,' said Ice, turning her blue eyes on him.

'Yes, about that.' Jack rubbed his wrists and nodded to the guard. 'Thanks, Wotsit.'

'Wepsit,' said the birdman steadily, but he didn't look too offended.

'Oh. Sorry. Must be the poison attack warped my brain a little.'

'You can call me Wotsit if you wish, Little Gold.'

Ozzy lowered his crook and flail and placed them on the floor so that he could pick up Jack's limbs in his long fingers and inspect him like a goat in the market. 'Yes. It is most unusual to be brain-warped only a little. The poison sac can indeed be used to good purpose, to treat the canker and the over-beating of the heart, but that must be in tiny amounts. The dose you received would floor a dromedary. They are hardy folk from the golden land from which you tarry, yes?'

'Not really,' said Jack, wondering where to start. 'And not really golden either. In fact, I'm sure the yellow is just sand.'

Ice laughed. 'But your hair is like corn growing in the fields under Ra.'

'Corn in the sun? I don't think so.'

So then she lowered her head so that he could see himself in the shiny disk between her cow horn headdress. At least, he hoped it was a headdress: it could be her actual Egyptian head. It was difficult to be sure in this place.

Jack inspected his head politely – 'Ah, yes. I can see why you might have thought I have golden hair' - and then shook himself like Roger after a wet day of grouse-hunting. Sand cascaded out of his ears and armpits, and he checked himself again. And then again.

'You're right! I've suddenly got fair hair. It must have been the journey here, or something. All that burning sun and whistling wind. Or the shock! I've heard of people turning silver after a horrible event. Maybe I've turned gold instead!'

It wasn't bright yellow as Ice had led him to believe, but it was certainly very fair. How the heck was he going to explain that to his parents? He'd need to have his hood glued permanently to his head! But then … perhaps his other head would look different now too. The doghead.

Which brought him back to Ozzy and Ice.

'Look, you were very kind not to kill me with the poison and all,' he said, 'but there's probably a reason I responded quite well to it. You see – and I know you'll understand this because of what you both are, too – I'm also a god.'

It was like being back on the sand dune. His comment was met with the same disbelieving silence as Ozzy, Ice and Wotsit exchanged glances and inspected him for signs of insanity, and then all three of them broke out into uproarious laughter.

'We said gold, not god!' gasped Ice, clutching her ribs.

Wotsit was sniggering through his beak in an extraordinary fashion. 'How can you be a god when you are so puny?'

'I'm not that puny, believe me.'

Ozzy hefted his crook above his head. 'All right, then, Little Gold. If you are a god, you can defend yourself against another god.' Then he cracked it down onto the sarcophagus, missing Jack's knee by the breadth of one of his golden hairs.

Time for them not to be golden any more. 'Okay, give me a second,' said Jack, holding up his hands.

Laughing, Ozzy pulled back the crook and waved to him. 'Please, do stand, oh great one.'

'Hm. You're a lot snarkier when you're a pharaoh,' muttered Jack under his breath, but he took the opportunity to drop down behind the marble plinth, wondering if this would be the only time his dog-head didn't pop up at the first sign of trouble. 'I am a god; focus and LOCK!' he told himself, picturing his muzzle growing outward, his ears rising to the top of his head in triangles, his teeth elongating and sharpening.

Not entirely sure that it had worked, Jack stood up.

Oh, it had definitely worked.

Ice's eyes nearly fired lasers at him when she saw what the transformation had achieved, and he noticed that she was now forced to look up at him. Ozzy, meanwhile, had picked up his flail along with his crook and was brandishing one in each hand, concern and not a little envy etched across his face.

Behind him, Wotsit gasped and dropped to one knee. 'My lord,' he whispered reverently.

'Oh, not you as well. I'm not,' groaned Jack. 'Not yet, at any rate.'

But on the whole, hearing it coming from Wotsit's ... well, beak ... and not spat out by Guisely, it did have a different ring to it.

Ice and Ozzy looked much less impressed than Wotsit, however. Both were circling him warily, Osiris with his flail aloft above his mighty head, ready to crack down on Jack's shoulders or curl themselves around his ankles to topple him to the floor. Nearby, Ice had lowered her cow horns like a bull preparing to charge, with every chance that she'd puncture both his lungs at once. Nice.

'Who are you, stranger?' hissed Ozzy, wielding the tip of his crook which suddenly appeared to be rather sharp. What would Albie have called it? An adze.

Ice gestured to Wotsit to tether Jack again, but the guard looked reluctant to tackle him. 'We are the ruling gods. Do you defy or usurp us?'

'No need for that. It's just me. Anubis some of the time, Jack Bootle-Cadogan most of the time.'

'We know not either of these names,' roared Osiris. 'What is your purpose for being here, Jackal-headed one?'

'I've come to find you,' said Jack simply. 'Like you came to find me, in the ...' Future. Maybe best not to say that. They were looking a bit agitated and he didn't want to find himself on the sharp end of a crook. '... desert,' he said instead. 'Surely you recognise me?'

'Before this rising of Ra we have never laid eyes upon you, imposter!' cried Ozzy.

'Never before!' Ice agreed.

'I demand of you on pain of death,' said Ozzy, aiming the razored tip of his crook at Jack's heart, 'that you tell us who sent you!'

'It was ...'

Wow. How did he explain this? It was you, actually, in a few thousand years' time. You and our mutual friends. Maybe the mention of their mutual friends would help!

'Amentet!' he cried hastily. 'Amentet sent me.'

'We know not Amentet,' snarled Ozzy.

'You do! Minty, with the hawk on her head and the shiny black hair ...'

Ozzy and Ice stared at each other.

'No. This is another of your stories. You have one last chance to tell us who sent you, Stranger with the Head of a Desert Dog, before we dispatch you to the afterlife!'

Wotsit had obviously considered his options and decided to join his master and mistress in the Jack attack. The three of them advanced, pinning him against the sarcophagus. They didn't know who he was. Or Minty. How was that possible? It was as if they didn't even exist yet...

And suddenly Jack realised his mistake. He *didn't* exist yet – not in ancient Egypt. Anubis was the son of someone or other, and presumably he hadn't been born yet. Amentet was probably in the same position. He was talking about the next generation of Egyptian gods, and the existing ones knew nothing about them.

He held his hands up. 'I can see this looks bad, but you have to trust me. I'm here for all the right reasons.'

The pointed objects pricked against his skin. Time for some quick thinking.

'I ... I tarry from the land of Little Golds,' he shouted hastily, 'as their ... representative!'

Yes, that sounded better than being a god. Jeepers, where was Albie when he needed him? He would know what to say. Jack shook his canine head as he tried to consider what Albie would do, and then on an inspiration, he dropped to one knee as Wotsit had done.

'I come to give our regards to the greatest Pharoah of all lands, including the land of Little Golds: England.'

'In-Gland,' repeated Isis hesitantly.

Jack shrugged. 'Yep. Close enough.'

'And who rules your In-Gland?'

'Well, actually we have a queen.' Jack paused, not sure how well this news would go down. 'She's been on the throne for over sixty years.'

'He means cycles,' said Osiris. 'Sixty cycles. Then she is a mighty and immortal ruler as we are.'

'She certainly is,' agreed Jack. No point in telling them at this stage that she wasn't actually going to live for ever.

Isis clapped her hands in delight, and Jack felt the frosty atmosphere melting. 'We love to hear of powerful queens! Is she a fair and just leader of her people? Does she ensure, as we do, that women and men are seen as equals?'

Jack nodded. 'Definitely.'

Isis was on a roll now. 'And does your queen insist that men cannot tell their wives or their daughters how they may attire themselves? I have just issued a decree to that effect. Issue it I have!'

'She is a powerful deity,' said Osiris, looking both humbled and pleased at the same time.

'Blimey,' said Jack. 'You should meet my mother. I don't think anyone would dare to tell her how to dress. And Minty would take your head off!'

'Then we are allies, Little Gold.' Osiris lowered the adze. 'We like the approach of your Queen and your In-Gland. And as her emissary, you must join us at our festivities this evening.

'Awesome!' Jack was so relieved he shrank back into his teenager form. 'When does it start?'

'Come,' commanded Osiris. 'It begins now.'

Isis smiled. 'Now it begins.'

Later, Jack was to realise that Isis had no idea how accurate her words were, but not in the way she'd anticipated ...

Chapter 7

The festivities were on a scale that Jack had never seen before, even at the glamping festival and Ed Sheeran concert they'd hosted at Lowmount the previous summer.

The venue reminded him of the cavernous ballroom in the Underworld, where all the Bas of the dead congregated before passing through to the Throne Room to be measured against the Feather of Thoth and – hopefully – to pass through to the Field of Rushes. He'd played basketball with the Ancient Dead Rellies there before now, and that was on a godly scale. Of course, as that was Ozzy's room too, it made sense that one was modelled on the other. Jack just wasn't sure, any longer, which one had come first.

The vast cathedral of a room into which he'd been led by Wotsit was pulsing with life in every corner, and all across the huge expanse of marbled floor, servants scurried with bowls from which grapes tumbled like waterfalls or aromatic stews steamed invitingly. Along one side of the hall was a row of spits over roaring fires; kilted chefs sweated and gleamed as they slowly rotated two dozen goats for the feast ahead. A small orchestra had already started playing in a distant corner, beyond the dais on which the thrones stood; before the musicians a phalanx of veiled women danced, telling stories with their hands and their hypnotic, swaying movements.

Jack's eyes fell upon the dais. There was Nephthys, watching him carefully out of the corner of her eye as she nodded to the music and the dancing women. At the far end of the dais, beside Ice's empty throne, sat someone far more interesting – and scary.

Seth slumped sideways in his throne, looking vaguely bored and passing a hand over his snouty face to smother a yawn. He nodded to a nearby acolyte who withdrew a pipe from the folds of his sleeve and began to play a strange, crooning melody. Immediately a large, flat head rose from the basket at the man's feet, followed by a slinky, sinuous body – a huge and dangerous cobra. The snake lifted from the basket until it stood practically on its tail, hypnotised by the tune issuing from the simple wooden flute, its head swaying directly in front of the man's face.

Jack glanced around, waiting for someone to stop the snake charmer before the cobra snapped out of its reverie, but everyone apart from Nephthys was transfixed by some other activity going on in the hall.

Knowing full well that Jack's eyes were upon him, Seth's pig-like face split into a horrible grin.

'Let it feast,' he said in a voice that Jack recognised only too well.

The snake charmer glanced at Seth, alarmed. 'My Lord Set, what do you mean?'

'You heard me,' sneered Seth. 'This endless swaying is tedious. Give it what it wants and let us have more entertainment.'

'Sir, I—'

Seth held up a hand. 'Stop. Playing.'

The man gasped at the same moment as Jack. The snake was wavering right in front of the charmer's face. If he ended the hypnotic piping from the flute, the snake would strike with one fatal bite.

Seth cold eyes met Jack's, and he was filled with horror. This was a direct challenge to him – interfere if you dare - and there was nothing he could do. He was a stranger in court, and a skinny teenager at that. Trembling, the snake charmer lowered his hands as if he himself was hypnotised, his head lowered to accept the inevitable blow about to penetrate the soft flesh of his neck ...

And just as the snake reared backwards, ready to lunge, someone stepped in front of Seth.

'Your king won't be happy if you keep killing the entertainment, Lord Set.'

It was Nephthys.

'Play.'

She waved to the charmer, who now had pearls of sweat rolling down his face. The instant he lifted the pipe to his lips and began to play, the cobra retracted its hooded head. Entranced by the music, it folded itself back into the woven basket, whereupon the charmer slapped on the lid and stood over it, head lowered, panting.

Seth glared at Nephthys. 'It was just a little fun, sister.'

'For nobody but you.'

Seth smiled evilly, and Jack knew at once what that expression meant. Nobody mattered but him. That was what he thought. 'Ah well. There'll be more fun for ... my king ... very soon,' he muttered through yellow teeth.

'What do you mean?' demanded Nephthys.

'It's a party. Organised by our Pharaoh. I simply meant that it will be fun for all concerned.'

'Right,' said Nephthys, as if she didn't believe a word of it. Then she saw Jack watching, and smiled. 'Our visitor. What think you of these celebrations?'

'Brilliant,' said Jack, and he wasn't lying, although he could have done without the snake attacks. It was true, though; it was an amazing event, and all around him the sound of hundreds or possibly thousands of people enjoying themselves with the soothsayers, the glorious food, the wonderful music lifted and swelled to fill the room.

'Come, sit at my feet,' said Nephthys.

Jack nodded towards his nemesis. 'I'll be seeing you later, Seth.' It was all Jack could do not to call him Pig-Face.

The man snarled. 'It's Lord Set.'

'Whatever.'

He wasn't about to start sucking up to the pig-headed one now. Perched on a stool beside Nephthys, Jack looked around as Big Ozzy and Ice made their way to their thrones, smiling and bowing to the revellers as they paraded through the party. Now that he'd seen the mood Seth was in, Jack had a very bad feeling about the whole thing. Thankfully the snake and its charmer had disappeared, so there was no threat there, and Ozzy and Ice were flanked by Wotsit and his host of hawk-headed soldiers. Surely no danger could come to them here ...

'Brother, Sister and son of In-Gland,' cried Ozzy as he approached the dais and plonked himself into this seat. 'Is this not the most marvellous of celebrations!'

'Fantastic!' said Jack. 'Though what are you celebrating, exactly?'

Ozzy and Ice smiled at each other. 'It has been a most mighty harvest along the life-giving Nile, and our people will eat well and prosper throughout the coming cycle. Our parents, the Earth God Geb and the Sky Goddess Nut, have blessed us fulsomely, and we give thanks to Atum, the creator of this world.'

'So it's a Harvest Festival. We have those too,' said Jack. 'In In-Gland.'

'Your queen honours her people. This we like,' cried Ice in delight.

At this, Seth stood up, and Jack felt a chill ripple along the dais. If he'd had his dog-head on, the fur on his neck would have bristled.

'We, too, honour our people and the Pharoah who leads them,' said Seth with a generous dose of slime.

'Why, thank you, brother.' Ozzy bowed his head graciously.

'In fact, I have a surprise for you.'

Ice clapped enthusiastically. 'We love surprises!'

'Love them we do,' Ozzy said with a grin. 'When can we see it?'

Seth paused as though he'd been planning to wait a while, then laughed, baring his vile teeth. 'All right, as you're so eager.' He rapped on the platform with his adze, and several bare-chested soldiers arrived. 'Bring the surprise!'

They all watched, open-mouthed, as the surprise was dragged before the dais.

It was a large wooden box, inlaid with faience, gold, amber glass and that strange silvery metal Jack had seen around the building. It was quite blindingly beautiful. The carvings of reeds waving at the edge of the water were so lifelike that they appeared to move, drifting this way and that as if caught in a gentle tide. When they magically reached out their fronds and slid the top of the box to one side, Jack caught his breath.

'Isn't that a ... coffin?' he whispered.

Beside him, Nephthys stiffened. 'Look about you, Little Gold,' she hissed, gripping the arms of her throne in alarm.

'Well, it is very lovely, brother,' Ozzy was saying, 'but what is the great surprise? Is it filled with debens?'

Seth laughed. 'Something much more precious. But you have to be inside it to see its gifts, for the answers are scribed inside the lid.'

'Oh no. I know your tricks,' said Ozzy, wagging a finger at Seth. 'I'll get in and you'll all run off and hide, as you did when we were children.'

'No, my lord, for you are now a mighty Pharoah. We shall all be right here as you discover the gifts of the magic box.'

Ozzy hesitated, looking amused, then stood up. 'Fine. I will play your game.'

'Don't!' shouted Jack, leaping to his feet. 'Don't get in there!' He looked around, panicking. He couldn't denounce Seth in front of everyone, but surely he wasn't the only one who could see that this was not going to lead to anything good. 'Let me get in!' he added abruptly.

Well, better him who distrusted Seth than the innocent Pharoah.

Unfortunately, his cry had the opposite effect to what he'd intended. Ozzy, sensing competition, skittered forwards with a holler of laughter and flung himself into the depths of the wooden crate. The reedy fingers eased the lid into position - Jack could still hear Ozzy's voice, confused, wondering where the clues and puzzles were inscribed – before the reeds knotted themselves into a tight rim and sealed the top of the coffin shut.

Because now there was no doubt that it was a coffin. A tightly closed coffin, containing Egypt's Pharoah.

Suddenly, Ozzy began hammering on the lid. 'Release me! There are no clues in here. What trickery is this, brother?'

'Goodness,' said Seth in a flat voice. 'I can't imagine where they've gone. Maybe the stranger in our midst has erased them.'

Jack held up his hands. 'Nothing to do with me.'

'I command you now, set me free!' Ozzy's voice was quavering a little, and he certainly wasn't laughing any longer.

Suddenly Ice screamed at the top of her voice and flung herself onto the lid. 'It's shrinking!' she howled. 'Stop it, brother! He will suffocate in there. There will be no air!'

'Oh, come now,' said Seth evenly. 'He's a great king. He must be able to get himself out of there.'

But Ice was right. The wooden sarcophagus was not simply a coffin. It was a murder weapon, getting smaller and tighter until it would surely squeeze the life out of Ozzy.

And before Jack, Nephthys and Ice could attempt to pry the lid open with an adze or even a scorpion tail, the reeds reached down to the floor to create a neat fringe – a fringe of tiny legs that turned the crate into an enormous centipede – and suddenly the coffin slithered out of the room, past the bewildered hawk platoon whose weapons achieved nothing, and out behind the palace where the Nile twinkled, beckoning its own reeds to its edges, and sweeping Ozzy into its swirling depths in the fatal grip of his own final resting place.

Chapter 8

'Brother, what have you done?' whispered Ice, her blue eyes turned almost white with terror and pain.

Seth jumped to his feet. 'What have I done? I was trying merely to entertain. I am as distraught as you at what has just happened. You would do better to suspect the stranger in our midst.'

Here we go again, thought Jack. He shook his head vehemently, half-expecting his dog ears to pop through his skull as his anxiety grew. 'I swear, Ice, it was all his doing. It's always Seth's doing. He's an evil pig.'

'Do not speak of Lord Set so!'

'I'm not calling him names. I mean literally – he actually is an evil pig. All this Lord Set business is just a cover-up.'

The queen's chips of ice turned on him, and he almost shivered. 'He is my brother, Little Gold of In-Gland, and you are no longer welcome here. Wepsit, despatch him!'

The bird-headed platoon swivelled as one and marched towards him.

'Ice, don't!' cried Jack. 'Let me be useful. I can go after Ozzy – I mean, Pharaoh.'

'I will seek the Pharaoh myself,' snarled Ice, more terrifying than Jack had ever seen her. 'You will be despatched.'

Wepsit had him by the arm. 'Just when I was starting to like you,' he said with a sniff, and then he opened his beak.

Jack stared into the cavernous hole, and felt a little faint. 'What the heck is that?' he croaked, pointing up to the Wepsit's beck as it descended towards his head.

'That, Little Gold, is my tominal tooth, the extended upper mandible of my beak,' explained Wepsit kindly, closing the offending beak as he spoke - to Jack's great relief. 'It fits into a notch in my lower mandible, and together they snap through a spine as easily as if it were an olive stone.' He clapped the two sections of beak together with the clatter of castanets, and they creaked like a set of nutcrackers. 'See?'

'You're going to snap through my spine?'

Wepsit shrugged. 'You are to be despatched in fair falcon fashion,' he said simply. 'Unlike most birds of prey who are do not maintain our high standards, we like our meat dead before we eat it. Don't worry – it will all be over very quickly.'

Jack closed his eyes, mostly to avoid the smirk on Seth's face as Wepsit primed his jaws, ready to slice through Jack's spinal column. Where oh where was Albie? Or Minty? He wasn't used to doing all this on his own. And then he thought of Ozzy, trapped inside a shrinking coffin that nobody was chasing. How alone must he be feeling – if he wasn't already dead.

Well, Seth wasn't going to get him killed too. Not until he'd had a good go at rescuing his friend.

'Sorry, Wotsit,' he said as the razor-sharp beak scratched against his neck. 'My spine's about to get a lot tougher to snap.'

He focussed and locked on his dog-self with more speed and concentration than he'd ever managed before, and to his joy he felt Wepsit's jaws glance off his shoulder and trail harmlessly down his arm as he shot outwards in both height and width. The crowds that had gathered when the coffin disappeared gasped in disbelief and then clapped enthusiastically, assuming this was part of the evening's festivities.

Jack gave a tiny bow as Wepsit and his henchmen scrabbled for their spears. 'Hey, if you like that, you'll love this,' he said.

He closed his eyes tight, picturing the sand dunes behind the palace, and zipped straight through Nephthys's throne, an orchestra which scattered at the strange whirlwind blasting through them, and out through the sandstone wall of the grand hall.

He'd hoped to reach the river straight away, but as he hadn't actually seen the Nile until he'd glimpsed it when the coffin danced through the doorway, he couldn't picture it as clearly as the sand dunes. In his haste, it seemed he'd imagined the sand dunes a little too well. As he opened his eyes, Jack found that his arms and hands were resting on the sand, with his canine head protruding above them as if he'd been buried from the neck down like some dad at the beach.

'I must look like the Sphinx,' he groaned, remembering the famous Egyptian statue that languished near the pyramids. 'Only in reverse.' The Sphinx, of course, had a human face and the body of a lion, and it was somewhere near the pyramids. But what pyramids? Once again, Jack realised that he hadn't seen a single one although he was in the Pharaoh's homeland.

And then a horrible thought occurred to him. What if there were no pyramids because Ozzy – the great pharaoh Osiris – hadn't survived?

He had to find him, immediately. A stampede of feet was thudding through the ground in which he was submerged, pointing to the imminent arrival of Wepsit and his terrible-toothed, falcon-headed friends. With solid ground no object to him, Jack centred his concentration on his recent sighting of the river, and ploughed through the sand towards the Nile.

The river into which he splashed was a vast waterway the width of a lake, festooned with fishing boats, handsome barques ferrying the wealthy to and fro, and livestock and people splashing at the water's edge. The reeds formed a thick barrier on one side – without his powers, Jack would have no chance of climbing out again – while the furthest bank was teeming with people. If Ozzy's impromptu coffin had washed up on that side, it could have been picked up by anybody.

Luckily, Jack knew Seth better than that. There was no way he would have imprisoned Osiris in so sneaky a fashion if there was a chance he'd escape within a few hundred metres – and anyway, that coffin could swim. Checking left and right, Jack decided that even a magical centipede of a crate would have struggled against the powerful current. He let himself be lifted by the water and struck out downstream, hoping against hope to find Ozzy before it was too late.

For hours he drifted, paddling into the reeds from time to time if he heard them rustle or to the bank if he smelt a fire. Each time, however, he would find only a nesting bird or a thirsty goat, or occasionally the smouldering remains of a campfire.

Once he scrambled ashore to follow a scent to find that the smell of burning was wafting out of a temple, where candles were lit along a low shelf in a way that reminded him of home. Painted on the wall in colours as bright as the people themselves were portraits of Ozzy and Ice – the King and Queen of Egypt. The room was empty apart from that, though, and Jack's heart sank as he made his way back to the river's edge. With dusk closing in Jack began to give up hope of ever finding Ozzy, or even seeing Ice again.

But suddenly there she was, as if she'd heard his thought, standing imperiously on a long, narrow boat in the shallows in much the same way he'd seen her take position on a flying camp bed.

'Ice!' he blurted out before he could stop himself.

The chilling blue eyes sought him out in the darkness. 'Is that you, Little Gold of In-Gland?'

Jack pushed through the reeds. 'I it is,' he said, feeling only a little foolish.

The Royal Barque bobbed against sinking sun, and the lengthening shadows made Ice appear to tower above him.

'I can't let you snap my neck, you know,' he said gruffly. 'I've got to find Ozzy.'

Ice sighed with that fractured wind that spoke of blizzards. 'My sibling has persuaded me of that.'

'Which one?' cried Jack, but before she could answer a figure stepped out from behind her.

Fearing it would be Seth, Jack plunged into the water, ready to swim or attack or rescue Ice, in whatever order might be necessary. Instead of the dreaded pig-face, however, he saw the graceful outline of Nephthys.

She reached out a hand to help him aboard the barque. 'Your powers are mighty, and we need to make use of them.'

Jack shook himself down with a canine body rotation that twisted him from the tips of his ears to his feet.

'Those are not the powers I mean, Jackal-Headed One, though the ones we require are those of the hound.' Nephthys gave him a tiny nod. 'We need your navigational and tracking skills.'

Jack sighed. 'I've been trying to track him down all day. Nothing so far.'

'Then try harder,' snapped Ice. Blimey, she was a lot bossier when she was a real queen.

'I'm trying as hard as I can!' Jack rounded on her angrily. 'Do you think I've been swimming around the Nile for a giggle? I need to find him too!'

He felt a gentle hand on his arm. Nephthys. 'We know you are trying, Jackal. But I think you are trying as your human self. We are more accustomed to our god-powers, and you must become so too. Have you been using your god-powers, Jackal?'

'Yes! I've been zipping and changing and—'

He stopped short, slapping a palm to his forehead. He hadn't, Jack realised, been using all of his god-powers. Dog powers, maybe, but not god-powers. He'd relied on his normal instincts to track Ozzy down, following clues of aromas and sounds, when all the time he could have been making all this a whole lot easier.

'I'm a dufus,' he said simply. 'Of course. I can use my god-powers to find Ozzy.'

'Then will you do it?' Ice looked at him fearfully. 'Wepsit and his team are our crew and they can force you if necessary, but I would wish for you to do it readily.'

'I do it completely readily,' said Jack. 'Wotsit can keep his mandibles to himself.'

'Thank you!' came a voice from the darkness. 'For I would derive no pleasure from killing you, and definitely none from eating you. You have a strange odour.'

Probably deodorant, thought Jack, or soap. He smiled at Ice as he considered his plan. 'I think I know what to do, but I've never tried it on water before, or with a boat.'

Ice bowed her head. 'We have powers of our own if you should struggle.'

'You certainly do. Right, then let's get on with it, shall we?'

The sisters nodded, resolute, and Jack gripped each of their shoulders. 'Oh, Wotsit,' he called. 'You'd all better hang on to me if you want to come with us.'

'As you say.'

The phalanx of falcon-headed soldiers stepped forward and formed a chain, hand-to-hand, with Wepsit's fist clamped firmly around Jack's neck in case he tried to escape. Ignoring the threat, Jack closed his eyes and remembered the last time he had seen Ozzy. Disappearing inside a coffin. Taking off inside a writhing wooden box that appeared to be alive. Getting smaller. Squeezing the life out of him as he was carried to the very river he was honouring ...

And with an immense wrench that felt as though he was sucking half the surrounding landscape along with him, some instinct within him pinpointed where his friend had disappeared to and surged towards the middle of the Nile.

Zipping was more difficult on water that on motorways, Jack discovered. The swirl of the river beneath him caused a whirlpool beneath the barque; the front end dipped alarmingly and then righted itself as the eddy spat them out on the other side upon a rising wave of black silted water. To Jack's astonishment and horror, rows of vicious teeth lunged at them through the uproar as crocodiles thrashed through the river, ripped into urgent activity by Jack's unusual travel methods. One or two were climbing aboard the barque; as he lashed out with his feet to push them back into the river, Jack feared he would let go of Ice and Nephthys.

Suddenly a voice spoke in his ear. 'Leave them to us, Little Gold,' said Wepsit. 'Now we can use our beaks to good purpose!' He laughed and motioned to his men, and they all cried out 'For Pharaoh!' as they lowered their adzes. The reptiles wouldn't stand a chance, thought Jack.

And neither would they, unless he sharpened up his tactics. The moment Wepsit let go of Jack's shoulder the barque powered forward again, surfing on a violent black wave that threatened to topple them into the gritty depths of the river. 'This is harder than I thought!' he shouted to the sisters.

Taking care not to twitch out of his grasp, Nephthys raised her arms: 'Becalm yourself, oh Nile! We mean you no harm,' she cried above the roaring wind. 'Simply take us where the Great Jackal requires.' Then she smiled at Jack. 'One of my powers – an affinity with rivers.'

Within moments the raging storm in the centre of the Nile had begun to settle, and even to be helpful. For a great distance the barque was able to plough along the river like a speedboat, with Jack and the two women leaning horizontally into the wind to stay aboard. Soon, though, Jack noticed that the landscape around them was changing. The banks were dotted with animals grazing in fields, and he could even spy the golden glow of a vast crop of wheat in the distance. Buildings were sprinkled and then clustered along the shoreline, and suddenly Jack could feel the barque turning in the river, directing itself towards a small jetty which led to a smattering of neat, white buildings.

The barque slowed to a halt and the trio jumped ashore. 'Where are we?' said Jack.

Ice looked around her. 'I believe we are in Byblos. Yes, over there is the palace of King Makande and Queen Astante.' She pointed to a distant building which appeared to be fairly grand, though not on the scale of her own palace.

'They may not welcome our presence, sister,' warned Nephthys.

'I care not,' said Ice sharply, 'if Osiris is here.'

At her words, Jack found himself thinking of Ozzy and the creeping coffin again, and without a moment to gather himself or take hold of the sisters once more, the ground ahead of him opened up into a channel through which Jack was suddenly forging, thigh-deep in dirt.

He zipped past straw-topped shacks and sturdier buildings; by market stalls and pools where women laughed as they washed their clothes, and into a huge field surrounded by tall trees, the like of which he hadn't seen so far in Egypt. This was obviously a very fertile part of the country.

And as for the god who would have created that good fortune – well, there he was. Or at least, there was the coffin, scuttling along on its horrid little reedy insect feet, straight towards a lone tree which dominated the centre of the field. It was taller than all the others, its branches reaching out to them all as if extended in friendship.

'Ozzy!' cried Jack, fixing his eyes on the slithering coffin so that he could zip to it more quickly.

It was nearly at the tree, and Jack feared that it would just keep running, on through the trees as they became a forest, with him always a field's length behind, never able to catch up with it, never able to thwart Seth's evil magic.

But then something far, far worse occurred. As the coffin raced towards the tree, the far-reaching branches stretched forwards, beckoning. This way, this way, they seemed to say. Then they touched the coffin, enveloping it, cradling it, lulling it to a gently stop before, to Jack's terror, hauling it towards the tree's own enormous trunk.

Unable to stop it, Jack could hardly bring himself to watch as a fissure ripped down the trunk of the great tree in the field's centre. It stretched and yawed, opening to display a dense, dizzying blackness, before the coffin was fed into the hole, sucked into the clenches of the tree trunk until it was no longer visible. And then, as if it had never been there at all, the tear in the tree's trunk merged like a zip, fading to a pale copper scar in the bark until it disappeared completely.

It was as if neither the terrifying mouth in the tree trunk, nor the coffin itself, had ever been there at all.

Chapter 9

The atmosphere at Jay's lodgings was even more rank and disgusting than the fetid ancient tombs into which Albie was accustomed to crawling. Unfortunately, this had nothing to do with the weather or the preponderance of fascinating artefacts, and everything to do with the way that Lord Jay Bootle-Cadogan had seen his girl twitched away from under his fabulously moustachioed nose, and by his own apprentice, no less.

Albie had excused himself from the Oasis Orchid as soon as it occurred to him that he was the only one who might be happy with Diselda's decision to give him her necklace. And even he wasn't especially happy – wasn't love meant to be delicious and rewarding? Shouldn't he be feeling on top of the world at this moment? He knew that Diselda the Dancing Darling would never go back on her word, having committed her 'heart' to him, and that knowledge should have made him delirious with joy. Instead he returned from the restaurant in the deepest of gloomy ruminations, hardly able to look at himself in the mirror as he splashed water from the basin onto his face, wondering the whole time how he'd made such a mess of everything.

Jay had stumbled back to the lodging house much, much later, cursing roundly as he stubbed his toe against the bed in the room adjoining Albie's. Albie listened fretfully, trying to decide whether he should knock on the door and try to explain himself, although he had no idea where he'd really begin. *Ah yes, Lord Jay; I'm actually a century old, returned from a future in which I have lived as a skeletal and mostly mute manservant to your wonderful wife and your bizarre offspring. Ta daaaa!* No, that wasn't going to work. He thought about it until Jay's fulsome snores rattled a thin piece of plaster off the wall, then he breathed a sigh of relief. It was too late, now, to say anything. To do anything. Too late for everything, in fact.

When he awoke in the morning, however, Albie felt filled with new resolve. It wasn't too late at all. It was actually quite the opposite. If anything, he was *early*.

After arranging with the concierge to send a trio of orchids to Diselda, insisting that they were from Jay and not from him, he set off with renewed vigour to find the one person in the souk who would understand (not including Minty, who would understand but not empathise at all).

He found Adjo asleep under his father's stall, cuddling the table leg tightly as if he was afraid of gravity disappearing.

'Adjo, wake up!' hissed Albie, stirring the boy's shoulder with his toe. 'I've stuffed up.'

Adjo sat bolt upright, instinctively missing the edge of the table as he blinked owlishly at the sun creeping up over the horizon. 'Master Cornthwaite. Ra's blessings upon you! What is stuffed up? You have a cold?'

'No, no, not that kind of stuffed up. I mean I've made a mistake, and I thought I'd created some terrible wrinkle in time but I've just realised that time is on our side, because we *know* everything ahead of it.'

Ajdo's brown eyes widened; grabbing his sandals, he scrambled to his feet and pulled Albie behind the canvas wall that protected the shoe-seller from the oils and flames of the lamp salesman on the next stall. 'So it is not a dream? I really am coming backwards from being forwards.'

'Yes,' said Albie. He leaned in closely. 'Last night I hinted to Diselda that I loved her and she gave me her heart on a string.'

'Agh!' cried Adjo, as if he'd been stung. 'But is that not Lord Jay's gift?'

Albie nodded, ignoring the hot flush along his cheekbones. 'Yes. I suppose so. I know she's incredibly fond of me and all that, but it's Jay she loves. Has loved all along. I don't know what possessed me, really. I just saw a chance and I took it.'

'Sometimes, my friend, you have to turn towards the opportunity that arises and trust that the gods have placed it there for you. That is all you did. And now it seems you reconsider. It is the wise man who can state that he has simply changed his mind since new information presented itself,' said Adjo solemnly. 'Do not look so startled,' he added in a whisper. 'You are not the only one who is actually over a century old. I am learning a few things about love and life, too.'

'Oh! Of course, I forgot,' said Albie, feeling a little clammy. It was a very strange conversation to be having with an Egyptian boy. But then it was a very strange set of circumstances all round.

'Anyway,' he continued, 'all that knowledge from being, as you say, a century old and so on – well, it isn't just about Diselda and affairs of the heart.' Albie pointed beyond the bazaar, out among the foothills where important archaeological digs were taking place. 'We know all about what's happening out there, too.'

'This is true!' squealed Adjo in delight. 'Ah, remember it all, Master Cornthwaite? How I tell you my name means "treasure" –'

'And I found the coffin with the name on it and knew it was what we had been looking for: the resting place of Osiris himself—'

'—that takes off like a great green caterpillar into the catacombs and leads you to Abydos—'

'—and the fountain of youth—'

'—before the great statue of Osiris which I am managing to destroy by disturbing you, so it topples into the waters and fills the lake and makes everything turn to dust!' Adjo ended triumphantly.

'Exactly,' said Albie. 'All of that. We know where the coffin is. We know where Abydos is. We know precisely and utterly where lies the greatest discovery in the whole of the history of mankind.'

Adjo's dark-rimmed eyes filled his entire face. 'Ohhhhh, that is very big.'

'It's perfect!' cried Albie, before Adjo clapped a hand across his mouth. 'Oh, apologies,' he mumbled through the boy's fingers. 'I was a trifle over-excited. Because it's perfect on two levels: on the one hand, I can lead Jay directly to a seventh wonder of the world and make him a hero—'

'—which will be the greatest moment to step aside graciously so he and Diselda can be together—'

'—and on top of all that—'

'We find Osiris!' they hissed together, jumping up and down with glee so that tiny eddies of sand swirled around their ankles.

'You really have become quite the wise old man,' said Albie with a touch of admiration.

Adjo grinned. 'Ah, am I not the greatest combination? The health and vitality of youth and the wisdom of centuries.'

'You are! We should bottle you and sell you in the souk!' said Albie with a laugh.

'Ha ha, yes! Essence of Adjo.'

The day was turning out to be much, much better than Albie could ever have hoped. After finalising his plans with Adjo, he collected warm, melting pastries from the bakery beside the spot where Minty and Diselda had met, hoping to see the not-so-friendly goddess and explain that he'd realised the error of his ways. There was something about her fierceness which he found oddly comforting. Knowing that Hathor might be about to pass on messages anyway, he directed his mouth to the sky and muttered the plan under his breath, ending, 'and I'm going to put it all right today. Right now, in fact. Even better than right, if that's possible.'

Because with all the knowledge he had to hand, Jay would survive. He would return with Diselda to Lowmount. They would dine out forever on fantastic stories of when Lord Jay Bootle-Cadogan found the god and pharaoh, Oriris, and Albie himself would be the dear friend in the background, craving neither the limelight nor the fortune, happy only to have played such an instrumental part in this monumental discovery.

He positively skipped back to the lodgings, planning his speech to Jay. 'Sorry, old chap; must have been the gin sling.' Or perhaps, 'Look, I do actually love her dearly but she only has eyes for you, and I can't get in the way of that,' or even, 'I know you'd win in a duel, whether it was pistols or rapiers, so I'm just going to back out before you kill me outright.'

Before any of that, however, there was something even more important to share with him. And it was lucky he was prepared for it, because there was Jay already, striding through the bazaar with a certain tinge of tetchiness in his confident step. He spotted Albie and made to turn away, then seemed to think better of it and strutted up to his apprentice instead.

'There you are,' he said evenly, not quite meeting Albie's eye. 'Planning on doing some work today? Or were you out early on a ... what would you call it ... an assignation?'

Diselda. He thought Albie had been out on some secret tryst with Diselda.

'No, of course I'm planning to work. I just went to ... to get these!' Albie held up the pastries, but Jay didn't look convinced or interested.

'You were a long time getting cakes,' he said with a sniff.

'Oh. Yes, I ... Well, the truth is,' stuttered Albie, 'I did actually have a meeting, but not the one you think. I was getting some very important information. Critical and immensely exciting information from a ... a source in the souk.'

Jay curled an eyebrow. 'A source in the souk? Sounds very reliable.'

'It is reliable. I know – *know* – that everything they said was true.'

'How?'

'Let's call it an instinct,' said Albie.

Jay was still glaring at him, but he could see that the man was intrigued. Nodding towards the coffee house, Jay hauled a seat beneath him and motioned to Albie to sit down.

Instead, Albie spoke directly into his ear. 'It's not safe to talk here. I think we should just go to the dig directly. Immediately.'

'But that'll mean another day's pay for the foreman and team,' said Jay with a frown. 'That's the last of the funding, old chap. Even lords can't live off their fortune forever, you know.'

And Albie crouched low beside his friend. 'But you will be able to, Jay. I promise you. For. Ever. Because I've located the resting place of Osiris.'

The explorer's expression froze, and Albie could see him doing mental calculations as the brilliant news sank in. 'We'll be covered for two hours,' he said finally as he stood up. 'And if you're wrong, you'll be getting a source in the dashed souk yourself. Do we understand each other?'

'I won't be wrong,' said Albie. He had never been more sure of anything. After all, he had time on his side.

They struck out for the dig immediately, Jay striding to the carts and camels with his usual commanding presence as Albie waved to Adjo to alert the foreman and workmen to their imminent arrival. They usually they went on foot but the excitement increased their urgency. They would go on four feet and a hump or two. The camel drivers would also need paying, but with the gold coins coming their way, there was nothing to worry about.

The thrill of being back on the dig site was so immense that it was all Albie could do to stop himself whooping aloud. Wiping sand from his spectacles, he gazed about him as the camel lurched towards the collection of small caves and hollows set into the dunes like so many hobbit holes. He was back. Back where he belonged, doing what he loved – what he had been trained to be. The hundred years of being a servant had not been awful in any way – he'd been with Diselda and then with Jack, after all – but this was the life blood that ran through his veins. Archaeology. Egyptology. Mummies and canopic jars, waving an adze and discovering ancient artefacts.

They had reached the lowest of the caves. Jay held a hasty interaction with the foreman, who, judging by the amount of wild hand waving that was going on, was not too pleased with doing yet more work when they hadn't been paid for the last couple of weeks. With a despairing glance at Albie – he interpreted it as 'You'd better be right or else' – Jay shook hands on whatever deal he'd just devised and waited for Albie to slide from the camel's back.

'Here we are then,' he said, shielding his eyes from the sun. 'So where to from here?'

Albie smiled, feeling as confident as he'd ever felt in his long, long, looooong life. 'We go through that second cave to the ante-room beyond.'

'After you,' said Jay. Then he smiled. 'If we've truly found Osiris, then it's your tip that's done it. You should be the first to see him.'

'Thank you.'

Albie stared at his friend for a moment, remembering how disarmingly nice he could be on occasions. Yes, he could also be sarcastic and sometimes full of bluster, but at his heart he was decent and kind. Jack clearly didn't just get those traits from Diselda alone ...

'This way,' he said, and hauled himself up the gritty slope towards the second opening, which he then widened with a pickaxe.

Through the entrance, the cave was gloomy and small. 'It's not very grand for a pharaoh, let alone for a god,' said Jay, barely able to stand straight in the opening.

'Ah. Well, you see - that's where we were going wrong.'

Albie looked about him, ready to point to a nearby coffin. To his surprise, the room was lined with stacks of jars and small wooden crates but otherwise it was empty. Perhaps his memory of it had been incorrect.

'Wrong?' repeated Jay.

Albie pulled himself together. 'Yes! We've been looking for a grand tomb fit for a leader, when in fact Osiris' resting place was a simple wooden sarcophagus, symbolising the agriculture of which he was god. The only clue to the coffin's content is the name on it: Adjo, meaning treasure.'

Jay lifted the lid of a nearby crate and stirred it with the tip of his finger. 'There's nothing regal in here. Just plates and household items.'

'Go through to the ante-room,' said Albie, with a growing sense of unease. This was definitely not how he'd remembered it. 'You'll see. The mummies are all in there.'

At that, Jay stood up straight and bumped his head on the ceiling. 'The what?'

'The mummies. Osiris and probably some of his entourage. Possibly his cat.'

Jay stared at him, his eyelids fluttering. 'Are you ... are you missing your mother, Albie?'

'No. What do you mean?'

'What do I mean? What do *you* mean? Why are you talking about mothers?'

Albie let out a hollow laugh. What a weird time to be joking. 'No, not mothers, Jay. Mummies. You know, bandages? Faience amulets and shabti statues to do the work in the afterlife? Canopic jars containing the organs?' Jay was looking at him as if he was mad. 'You do know ... Mummies, Jay! Embalmed bodies wrapped in linen and encased in wonderfully decorated sarcophagi?'

Jay passed a hand over his face. 'Albie, dear fellow,' he said after a moment, 'I haven't the faintest idea what you're talking about.' He appeared to be completely genuine. He was even looking at Albie with concern, as if he might have sunstroke or dengue fever.

Feeling a similar concern for his mentor, Albie laughed. 'I know you're playing some prank on me, Jay. Why else would we be here? What have we been searching for all this time if not for mummies?'

'For a headstone,' said Jay quietly, almost gently. 'For a grave or a memorial or hieroglyphs or something to show where Osiris was buried.'

'But here's where he is. Mummified! In his simple wooden sarcophagus, through here,' cried Albie, and he ran as fast as the crumbling, shoulder-height ceiling would allow to where he knew they would find what he had discovered before: the resting place of Osiris, there among the other coffins and sarcophagi, appearing to be the most insignificant of all the mummies there but really the most amazing discovery of all time.

He stopped short in the cave, peering into the corners. 'It's ... it must have been raided. I don't understand, it can't have been, because it was all here and I found it before ... the other time ...'

Apart from a rat's nest in the corner, and a jar that clearly contained wine and not any kind of human organ, the space was completely empty.

'This just isn't possible,' he groaned plaintively. 'I don't understand, Jay.'

'Neither do I.' Jay was surveying the empty room with a hand across his heart, as if it physically pained him. 'First Diselda and now this? I can't believe how much faith I put in you, for you to ... do this. How could you? If you deliberately set out to ruin me, Albert Cornthwaite, then you've done an excellent job.'

Throwing him a look of disgust from which Albie thought he might never recover, Jay wrenched himself out of the anteroom and made for the main doorway.

'Where are you going?'

A long dark shape fell across the cave as Jay turned at the entrance. 'The Oasis Orchid. The Black Diamond Poker Game starts in two hours. I'm going to do whatever I can to win back the fortune you just lost me.'

Albie started to protest, to try to warn him, but Jay held up a large hand to stop him in his tracks. The shadows extended like snakes around the cave walls.

'And this time, Albie,' he ended softly, not letting Albie continue, 'don't even dream of following me.'

Albie watched Jay disappear over the saddle of sand between them and the town, his heart feeling as shrivelled and calcified as the one that should have been in Osiris' chest. He leaned in the cave doorway, trying to figure out what must have happened, and then when he realised he must have gone into the wrong cave, he ran from aperture to aperture in increasing despair, tearing at the cave entrances with his pathetic little trowel, and then his bare hands, only to find there was nothing of note in any of them – only household items that the locals appeared to be storing in their cool depths.

'No!' he screamed as the last known cave offered up the same sad contents. 'It can't be! You have to be here, Ozzy. You have to be!'

At the sound of his voice, Adjo raced up the slop towards him, nodding to the foreman to show he would deal with it.

'You have not found the treasure?' he hissed. 'I saw Lord Jay stamping back into town like an angry lion.'

'It's not here, Adjo.' Albie ran his hands through his wild hair. 'None of them are here. How can this be? We know this is even before the exact moment I discovered it the first time, and there were several other mummies in the second cave alone.'

'They have been stolen, perhaps?'

'No, because then I wouldn't have found them the first time around. And there's another thing,' said Albie, remembering Jay's strange reaction. 'Lord Jay didn't seem to have even heard of mummies, let alone be looking before one.'

Adjo laughed in disbelief. 'Not heard of mummies? Who has not heard of the mummies of Ancient Egypt? The famous embalmed bodies, with their organs in jars and treasures all around to assist them in the after-life?'

'I know.'

But the boy hadn't finished. 'Who has not heard of the magnificent ceremonies with the weighing of the soul against the Feather of Thoth, and the passing through of the Ba to the Field of Rushes to be with the great god Osiris for all eternity?'

'I know, Adjo.'

'But who, seriously, who would come to Egypt on an archaeological dig if not to find a mummy?'

'Adjo, you're preaching to the Egyptian choir. I know all of this, but suddenly it seemed as if Jay didn't have the first clue about mummies.'

And then he remembered his Egyptian mythology, and a cold hand clenched around his gizzards. 'Oh my goodness,' he said, feeling his thin moustache prickle with sweat. 'It's ... it can't be. Adjo, who was the first mummy to be created?'

The boy grinned confidently, but then the smile faded. 'Oh, Master C. The first mummy was the great lord Osiris.'

'So if he was never mummified, it's possible there would be no mummies in Egyptian history, yes?'

Adjo nodded bleakly.

'And why would he not have been mummified?' continued Albie, almost to himself.

'Either because they couldn't find him at all and Seth got his terrible, terrible way—'

'—or because the person or god responsible for mummification didn't ever invent it.'

Their eyes and voices met in fear as they realised what all this pointed towards. 'Jack.'

Chapter 10

Jack banged on the tree's trunk. 'Open up!' he shouted in as commanding a voice as possible, which wasn't very commanding at all. He sounded like a schoolboy playing a policeman in a school production. Clearing his throat and trying a deeper pitch, he pounded on the bark again. 'Come on. Spit him out!'

The tree didn't seem to be in any danger of complying any time soon. In fact, it looked so much like an ordinary tree that Jack almost doubted what he had seen. Then, to his relief, he found that he hadn't been alone while it happened. On the other side of the tree and further towards the rooftop of the palace at the end of the field, a rather grand picnic was taking place.

Maybe these people had seen the tree swallow Orisis, although they were so engrossed in their festivities that Jack suspected this might be wishing for the impossible. Two thrones rather like Ozzy's had been set upon the grass with their backs to the tree, so Jack couldn't see who was on them. On the many colourful rugs and low copper tables before them, however, was a feast that would have made his father happy, supplied by long-gowned servants who wafted among the furniture like ghosts to a bevy of laughing children and adults. A boy of about three was having a hilarious time, watching nuts arc through the air from one of the thrones before scrambling into position to catch them in his mouth. Raucous laughter ensued from the seats each time he managed to snaffle one up.

But they couldn't all be watching the boy. Surely someone had seen something? Checking first that he had his human head in place, Jack was just about to approach them when a cold hand thumped down on his shoulder.

'Why did you leave us?' cried Ice indignantly. 'The border men were furious and made us explain ourselves. And we are queens!'

'I didn't mean to, honestly. I just thought about Ozzy – your Lord Osiris – and suddenly here I was in this field.'

Nephthys looked as calm and warm as her sister was icy, with her chestnut brown hair and kind eyes. 'We are in a different country now,' she explained. 'The Phoenician Guards welcome Egyptians, especially royal deities, but not if they do not announce themselves first.'

Jack shrugged helplessly. 'I'll go back and explain myself to them, I promise. But I'm so glad you're here because I know where the coffin is.'

Ice's face lit up with joy. 'You have it? Then why are we wasting time in discussion? Let us release Osiris!'

'I don't exactly have it,' said Jack. He pointed to the tree behind him. 'It's in there.' And he described what he had seen to the sisters, who listened with increasing levels of agitation.

'But I would feel his presence here, I am sure of it. Are you telling us your tales again, Little Gold?' said Ice, clearly starting to panic in a way that Jack recognised.

'Fear not, Sister. We shall find him.' Nephthys turned to the tree as Jack had done. 'Dear Cedar of Lebanon, we admire your greatness in height and breadth and beauty, and most of all your kind protection of our King. But now that we are here, would you be so gracious as to release him from your depths?'

'I tried that already,' said Jack, although he had to admit that 'Spit him out' probably didn't have quite the same ring.

The tree didn't seem to care either way. It stood as mighty and unmoving as ever, making Jack's story sound so implausible that he didn't wonder that Ice didn't believe him.

'We'll figure it out,' he said, just as a small boy pelted around the vast circumference of the tree trunk and cannoned into him.

It was one of the children from the festivities – the nut-catcher. He'd obviously run to catch a high-flung nut and kept running. In his surprise at bumping into Jack, he let out a yelp and promptly got the nut caught in the back of his throat. The cry turned into a cough and then a hideous wheezing sound, and to his alarm, Jack could see the boy's spirit beginning to separate from his body.

'He's choking to death!' Jack cried. 'Someone has to do that manoeuvre thing on him – you know, where you grab him from the back and crush his ribs.' He'd never done it, of course, but he'd seen it in enough films to feel that he could have a good go at it.

Before he could test his theory, however, Ice swept the child up in her arms, just as the nut-throwers and a whole host of the picnic party appeared.

'Little one, it is not your time,' she said gently. Then she eased open his mouth and projected a tendril of swirling white from the tip of her finger down his throat. Withdrawing her hand slowly, she drew the icy string back towards her finger. On the end of it was the dangerous nut. The boy blinked in surprise and then let out a wail so loud that there could be no doubt there was plenty of air getting to his lungs.

'Oh, well done, Ice,' said Jack. 'That was probably better than the rib-squashing thing.'

'Ice?' The boy's father rushed forward, reaching for his son but bowing at the same time so that he almost staggered into them. 'Queen Isis, that must be you for such a miracle to have saved my son's life?'

'I it is, King Malacander, along with my sister Nephthys and ... our manservant, Little Gold.' Ice handed the boy over and nodded graciously, her horned headrest glinting. 'My apologies for intruding on your festivities.'

'Intruding? Queen Astante and I could not be more grateful for your presence! Without it, we would have lost our most precious creation.'

The boy had recovered to the extent that he was pawing through his mother's pockets in search of the next nut, and as he was picking his nose in the meantime he didn't look quite so precious any more. Finding a large walnut in his mother's robes, the boy stared at Jack for a second and then, very deliberately, threw it at him.

Ice simply smiled. 'I'm glad I was here at your service,' she said, 'and now perhaps you will be of assistance to me, for I come in great need of it.'

The king knelt at her feet. 'Goddess, you shall have all my attention to whatever your heart desires. Come now to the palace and rest and eat with us, and then we shall bring all the wealth, knowledge and power of the might city of Byblos to your aid.' Waving to his manservant, he continued, 'But first! This miracle tree from which you sprang to save my beloved child shall be cut down and brought to the palace too, to remind us of your goodness for the rest of our days!'

'A grand idea!' his wife agreed. 'We shall create a pillar from this magnificent trunk, and forever will it hold aloft the roof of the palace courtyard, protecting us from the elements as you have protected us from ourselves.'

'Um, I don't think it is such a grand idea,' said Jack hesitantly. With Ozzy buried within it, it might be the fact that the tree was rooted into the earth that was keeping him alive. If he was alive.

But Ice shook her head slightly. 'Quiet, manservant,' she said softly, before turning back to their hosts with a fixed smile.

'You are most gracious, your majesties,' Nephthys interjected. 'But may we urge you to act in some haste, before our situation becomes dire.'

Ice nodded. 'Dire it will become.'

Dire it might well become if you keep calling me manservant, Jack thought venomously, but even he could see that Nephthys' fluid way with words was having more effect than anything he might do. As a team of workmen with blocks, tackles and enormous saws appeared out of nowhere to topple the tree, Jack fell into step behind the royal party, recognising fully for the first time in his life what it might feel like to be Bone. Where was Albie now? Wherever it was, he hoped he was having more luck than Jack was at tracking down their mutual friend, Green Ozzy.

The only thing was, he discovered the next morning, Green Ozzy was most definitely there with them in the palace of King Malacander and Queen Astante.

Rather to his shock, while the royal party feasted and swapped stories, Jack had been banished to the children's wing to entertain the horrible royal offspring, which included some equally spoilt twin girls who were a little older than the boy and wanted to dress Jack up and put black kohl round his eyes. When they got too much for him he quickly transformed into his dog-headed self, and suddenly they screamed in triplicate and ran outside to tell on him.

The more he discovered what Bone's life had actually been like, the less he liked it.

Later he had been invited into the servant's kitchen and given a perfectly nice meal of some kind of lamb stew with rice and fruit, before being ushered to a dorm room of twenty or more low beds made from rushes. He spent the night tossing uncomfortably and listening to the men who'd had to erect the tree in the palace courtyard complain about their aching muscles. He didn't fully understand what they were saying, but he was pretty sure from some of the mimes of coughing up walnuts that they shared Jack's view of the king's children and didn't appreciate having to create monuments to them.

In the dawn's weak light, Jack followed the scent of the tree to the courtyard in which it stood, no longer a magnificent cedar with its great outreach of branches, but instead a supporting pillar in the centre of the open space, holding up the apex of the roof. Jack could hardly imagine how many men it had taken to get this all prepared and in place over just one night. Still, if Ozzy had been able to help, Jack was sure he would have done whatever he could to make the task as easy as possible for everyone involved.

As he thought with a pang about his friend, a face appeared in the pillar before him.

'Ozzy! You're okay!'

Jack rushed forward to pull Ozzy out of the trunk, but Ozzy's face creased in concern and then evaporated before he could reach him.

'No! Come on; I'll get you out.'

This time Ozzy's head and shoulders emerged from the pillar, higher up this time and not quite so solid-looking. To Jack's dismay, this Ozzy seemed to be more ghost-like than physically formed. This was his Ba appearing, which meant that time really was growing short. They had to get him out of there. Ozzy's face was changing by the second, from smooth and innocent to wizened and ancient then back again. His shoulders turned towards Jack, appealing to him, begging him to get him out, but as soon as Jack touched the trunk he disappeared again, not able to maintain his extension from the heart of the trunk if Jack was in contact with it.

The palace rumbled into life around Jack, with girls arriving to sweep the edges of the courtyard while the cascading plants on the walls were watered. He knew that he would have a very limited time to do anything before Ice got swept up into the royal routines without speaking to him first. He had to find her now.

There was only one way to do that quickly. It was definitely a time to use his god-powers.

Hiding behind the pillar, he transformed from Little Gold – 'Jack!' he reminded himself – into Anubis. Next, he centred his thoughts on Ice as he had seen her the day before: a little frosty towards him, still slightly suspicious of his motives, perhaps. Closing his eyes, he remembered her rescuing King Malacander's son with her frozen finger and immersed himself in the feeling of her presence.

Suddenly it began, the curious lurch in his gut as he began to travel to an unknown destination, almost as if he was being pulled along by an invisible rope like the thread from Ice's fingertip. He passed straight through the pillar, sensing the green newness of the wood, then in and out of another and two further struts until he reached the edge of the courtyard. Careering to the right, Jack shot through the kitchens at lightning speed to the row of low buildings behind the palace, where he slid to a halt before a shuttered window.

'Thank you, powers,' he said under his breath. Without them he could have been searching the palace for hours, little knowing that there was some kind of guest annexe out the back.

He could hear Ice and her sister engaged in a heated argument behind the shutters.

'But he is a stranger!' Ice was saying. 'Why should I believe him?'

Ah. Him. They were discussing Jack.

Luckily, Nephthys seemed very much on his side. 'You have nobody else to trust but me, sister,' she replied evenly. 'And he seems genuine to me. He cares about Osiris.'

'Um, hello?' called Jack, not wanting to pry any more.

Or hear what Ice thought of him.

The shutters flew open and Ice's head appeared. 'See, Sister? He spies on us.'

'Spy on you I don't,' spluttered Jack. 'Why would I announce myself if I was spying on you?'

Ice stared at him for a moment and then shrugged. 'That is true,' she conceded.

'True it is,' said Nephthys behind her.

Jack smothered a laugh. 'Blimey, you both do it! Anyway,' he continued hastily, 'we have to do something quickly. Ozzy is definitely in the tree because he just tried to climb out of it. Trouble is, the tree is now holding up the palace courtyard roof.'

Ice sighed with a chill like the north wind. 'I know not what to do. King Malacander is ready to gather troops on my behalf and go to war if Lord Set is indeed behind this as you and my sister believe. Surely that is the way to go? We must march on Egypt to save our kingdom from a usurper.'

'No way!' Jack could hardly believe what he was hearing. 'War instead of having a go at releasing Ozzy? We have to at least try to get him out first!'

'I agree with Little Gold,' said Nephthys, 'who at this moment is neither Little nor Gold. But perhaps this is the way,' she added thoughtfully.

'I must do something. Anything to save Osiris before it is too late!' cried Ice – and Jack could hear it in her voice. She was losing it. She'd be wailing and thrashing soon if they didn't do something quickly.

It was time to act first and regret it later. 'Nephthys, when you said this is the way, did you mean me being big?'

She nodded.

'Okay. And you're obviously a tree yourself, judging by how you appeared to me at Lowmount.'

'Not that particular tree,' said Nephthys. 'I am a sycamore.'

'Ah yes, the sycamore sisters.' They'd made an appearance the previous summer to help Ice out, and Jack remembered their tall, graceful swaying. 'Then that's what we need to do. Ice, you go and talk to Malacander about gathering troops if this doesn't work, and meanwhile your sister and I will try to save Ozzy.'

As Ice hurried away to the royal chambers, Jack ran back to the courtyard with Nephthys right beside him. He was amazed at her speed given that she was his mother's age - but then, she was a goddess, and that made her very useful in all sorts of ways.

They arrived in the courtyard not a moment too soon. Ozzy's top half was hanging from the pillar, arms dangling down and head drooping like a dying orchid.

'Do you see him?' whispered Nephthys.

Jack nodded. 'We're losing him. We have to do this now.'

'On your command.' She seemed to know instinctively what he had planned, which was pretty amazing, given that he was making it up as he went along.

'Okay. I'm going to move him, then you'll have to take my place. Ready?'

On her nod, Jack placed himself squarely in front of Ozzy. 'I'm getting you out of there, Oz. Just hang on and you'll be back with us before you know it.'

The dangling form of his friend stirred slightly, and for a split second Ozzy seemed to smile, but then he faded into a mist the colour of a spring leaf and was sucked back within the pillar.

'Don't fail me now, god-powers,' muttered Jack.

He placed his hands as far as they would reach around the trunk's enormous circumference, and breathed in. He had to reach for a different part of himself, some element of his powers that he hadn't fully accessed before. In his mind's eye, he visualised himself at the top of the pillar, while at the same time he pushed his feet firmly against the marbled floor of the courtyard. The wrenching motion in his stomach fizzed into life, but to Jack's delight he felt it go up and down his body instead of stretching out before him. His hands were sliding up the tree's smoothed sides, rippling over the hastily-added carvings and decorations as his tendons and limbs and torso stretched beyond all imagination. Suddenly his fingertips touched and interlinked behind the pillar. Now he could reach all the way around it! And as he felt his canine ears touch something cool, Jack opened his eyes.

'Nicely done, god-powers!'

He was completely enormous. His head reached the courtyard roof, and each one of his shoulders could have taken out a neighboring pillar if he just shoved a little. The pillar, formed from the gigantic tree he had seen the day before, was now nestled in his arms like a log, as if he was about to engage in the Highland sport of caber tossing that his father had insisted they do at New Year's. It was exactly as he'd hoped for, and now he had to make the most of it. The strain of his vast head against the tiled roof was already causing cracks to form in the plasterwork, and a pillar ahead of him was working itself loose of its footings as if an earthquake was rattling at it.

'I'm going to move the pillar,' he whispered to Nephthys, realising that his voice was also enormous and could make the building crumble on its own. 'Hold everything up!'

'Always,' replied the goddess enigmatically, as her chestnut tresses wound out to form branches and down to encompass her body until it became the trunk of a glorious sycamore. She held out her arms; like fairylights, tiny leaves blossomed along the branches and twinkled into life as foliage filled the top of the courtyard.

The second her bark-covered hands were on a level with his face, Jack gripped the pillar tight and leaned against it. The foundations groaned ominously and around him, tiles clattered and crashed to the floor.

'I have it, Jackal,' said Nephthys as servants screamed, running to escape the falling debris. From each of her fingers and even her thumbs, green fronds curled forth and then unfurled at an enormous rate, knotting and lacing themselves in to a lattice that stretched across the entire roof, holding it in place as Jack removed the central support.

'Now!' he cried.

He pushed as hard as he could, feeling the timber splitting away from the coils of iron holding it in place at floor-level. The top of the pillar had been slotted into a quickly constructed ring of plaster decorated with gold. The whole thing slid aside as the pillar creaked sideways, cradled in Jack's vast arms. He stepped aside and laid it on the floor, at the very same moment as Nephthys swayed into position in the centre of the courtyard.

'Go! Release him from his prison.'

'I don't actually know how to,' said Jack.

'Yes, you do. Deep down, you do.'

The goddess smiled at him, more confident of his abilities than he was. Jack sighed, then shouldered the section of pillar that was left and staggered from the courtyard. He was getting smaller, and thought he was still powerfully god-like, the weight of a whole tree would flatten him if he tried to drag it along.

Once again, though, he remembered that he didn't have to do anything so boringly human, or even inhuman.

'River!' he told himself sharply, taking a tight hold of his prize.

Chapter 11

In nanoseconds he was on the banks of the Nile, even though he'd been told by a manservant that they were many, many miles from it. Distance and time – and size – were becoming less of an issue for him the more accurately he used his powers.

In the east, the sun was rising into a deep blue sky. Gone was the wispy greyness of dawn. This was something magnificent and primal. 'Ra in you, Ozzy,' said Jack, rolling the pillar into the water.

Brilliant rays of sunlight touched the tree's surface, and suddenly the process that Jack had witnessed went into reverse. Down the centre of the trunk a split appeared, widening and stretching as if the tree itself were yawning and awakening in honour of a new day, and all at once, Jack let out a gasp. There was the coffin, nestled in the very epicentre of the tree, only now it didn't look like a coffin. It was more like a hammock, containing the peacefully sleeping body of Osiris.

'Finally!' cried Jack. 'We've been looking everywhere for you.'

To his surprise, however, Ozzy didn't awaken and speak to him directly. Instead, his ba rose out of his chest, sitting upright and stretching his arms towards the glowing disc of sunlight above. 'Ah, that feels good. Ra in you, Jack.'

Jack stared at Ozzy's ba, confused. 'Why are you in two bits?'

His friend smiled gently. 'Only two? I am soon to be in more bits. There is more to be done, Little Gold.'

'You remember all that?' said Jack with a laugh.

'I remember it all now, Jack.' Ozzy looked down on his own sleeping body. Was it actually sleeping? Jack wasn't sure. 'Remember it all I do.'

'What do you mean?'

And Ozzy pointed along the river. 'They come.'

Jack looked around. There was Ice, at the head of a wave of soldiers, Wepsit and his troop among them and with King Malacander at her side. When she saw Jack, she raced to a barque and headed out to the centre of the river to join them.

'She must have used many of her powers to gather an army and rally them at this point so quickly,' said Jack to Ozzy.

'Powerful she is,' agreed Ozzy's spirit. 'As is he.'

'Who? Malacander?'

Ozzy shook his head sadly. 'My brother.'

Jack swivelled around as fast as he could to view the other bank, his heart sinking even as he turned. He had known in his heart that Seth wouldn't give up easily, but somehow he'd persuaded himself that finding Ozzy would be enough. He'd located him, for sure, but he wasn't quite convinced that Ozzy was all there. He seemed to be in spirit form only.

Meanwhile, on the shore opposite the modest army of Malacander and Ice stood the terrifying form of Lord Set. He looked almost casual, there on his own, apparently bored and unconcerned that he was about to be mown down by a bunch of soldiers.

Ice appeared at Jack's side, gazing into the tree's depths with tears glittering in her eyes.

'My Lord Osiris.' She gasped in pain. 'We are too late!'

'No, he's still here. Really chatty. Right here. Can't you see him?' Jack pointed to where Ozzy was now sitting on the edge of the cleft in the tree trunk, kicking his legs about carelessly.

Casting around her desperately, Ice looked for Ozzy but to no avail. 'Does he sleep? Or is it what I fear?'

Ozzy's ba smiled sympathetically at Jack, with a look that said 'Explain this one, mate.'

The truth, though, was that Jack didn't really know the answer. 'I'm not sure,' he said carefully. 'He's still very much here to me, but if you can't see him then I don't know.'

He felt Ice's fingers on his arm, gripping like a vice. 'My powers are great, Little Gold. If he is more than asleep, then I will bring his body back to life, as surely as Osiris brings the Nile back to life each Day of Ra.'

It sounded weird and impossible, thought Jack. But then, if someone had told him any of this would be possible – that he could zip and grow to the size of your average tower block – then he wouldn't have believed them. Maybe this had been what Ozzy was waiting for. To be found. To be brought back to life by Ice.

But just as Ice reached out towards the body in the coffin, from across the river came an insidious roar like the splitting apart of a human torso. It was like nothing Jack had ever heard before, despite being in the vile presence of Seth as his pig-self on various occasions. He turned to warn Ice, but it was too late.

The roar had not simply been a shout of anger, although that was certainly part of it. It had been a call to action.

Ploughing into the river with a presence that could have turned back oceans was a hideous sight: a terrible, mammoth-sized hippopotamus, slavering and ponderous, ruby-scarlet against the backdrop of the sun. As the gigantic head with the familiar porcine eyes lowered into the Nile, the river stirred and bubbled as if it were boiling. Into its sulphurous depths the animal plunged. Before they could even form a response, it was upon them, tearing at the tree trunk, splintering the wood in is enormous jaws as if it were sugar strands. Jack tried to focus on becoming a giant again but the speed and relentlessness of the attack was overwhelming; he was thrown to one side like ragdoll, leaving Ice unprotected.

Her army sprang into action, Wepsit and the hawk-men swooping and crying with their strange metallic adzes aloft, as the soldiers of Byblos followed their king through the reeds towards Ice's barque. But they had reacted too slowly, and already the hippopotamus' hideous mouth had reached the body of Osiris. Jack scrambled and thrashed through the water as Ice screamed out to her soldiers to help her, but Jack knew it was too late.

Ozzy knew it too. His ba stood silently on the remains of the trunk, looking directly at Jack. 'Remember why we came to you,' he said suddenly, in a voice that Jack could hear inside his head even though Ozzy was metres away.

The hippo crashed down on the bobbing pillar, now shredded and in ruins. Ozzy's ba closed his eyes and vanished, and at the very moment Seth's teeth touched the coffin, the body solidified into deep green marble. No, not marble. Jade, Jack realised – like the statuette of Ozzy they'd found in the British Museum. As the head of the monstrous river creature made contact with the jade, the body cracked along the middle and shattered into many pieces, some rolling away down the side of the plunging tree trunk, others embedded more deeply within it.

Ice's scream became a soul-rending wail, so heartbroken that hailstones began to rain down on the African river.

Not finished even now it had destroyed Osiris, the creature reared like a stallion, its underbelly a swarming, writhing nest of cobras and asps. It brought both feet down into the river bed with a stamp that shuddered like a thunder clap.

And then Jack saw it forming – the tidal wave that Seth had created.

The flood swept in a torrent across the Nile, taking everything and everyone with it, even Jack with his own god-powers. Clinging to the tree in her torment, Ice didn't even defend herself against the deluge, racing along on the crest of the tsunami-like wave until she plunged out of sight near the city. As for the army – Jack could only hope that they'd managed to get to the barque or into the sky (if the falcon-men could indeed fly), because there was no sign of any of them.

The only person – no, thing – remaining was Seth.

The blood-coloured carcass of the hippo stomped towards him.

'You will not beat me, Head of Dog,' snarled a horribly familiar voice.

'Watch me,' replied Jack, 'Head of Ugly.'

'Oh, believe me, I will. As you fail. And as I take over from my brother, you can watch me.'

Jack attempted a laugh. 'But he's still here. Still Pharaoh.'

'Where?' The monster looked around, mocking. 'Where is the great Osiris?'

'He's ... I'll find him,' said Jack defiantly.

'No,' said Seth. 'You will fail. It is done.'

And as the hippo clambered onto the bank and turned back into a throne-usurping monstrosity of a man, Jack suspected that he was right.

Because he knew what Ozzy had meant when he'd uttered his last words: 'Remember why we came to you, Jack.'

He still didn't have it. What they first came for. He could find all the parts of Osiris, using his god-powers to track down all the parts of the statue that had tumbled into the water, but he still didn't have what they first came for.

He was still missing a piece of Osiris, and without it they could do nothing.

They still had to - had to – find Ozzy's missing crown.

Or Seth had won.

With a sigh, Jack waded back to the water's edge, wondering what on earth he'd done to deserve all of this. The curse that had been laid upon his family had become a never-ending nightmare.

Chapter 12

Using the cursed dog-god powers, Jack found Ice and Nephthys sloughing through the Nile a mile or two from where they had been swept away. Both sisters were trying not to cry as they studied whatever Ice was cradling in her arms, and Ice's tears had created a frosty frill along the banks of the river.

As Jack zipped through the reeds, Ice turned towards him sadly so that he could finally see what she was holding. It was a foot – Ozzy's hard, green foot that had broken off somewhere above the ankle. It looked like the Grinch's sock, but Jack stopped himself from pointing this out. It was hardly the time for jokes, and besides, he was in Ancient Egypt where they'd never heard of the Grinch. The nearest they came to weird hairy human characters was ... well, him.

'It is all we have managed to locate,' said Nephthys gently, her eyes warning him to take it easy. Ice was in a delicate state.

Jack nodded as he carefully focussed on becoming his teenager self. 'How did you find it?'

Both sisters pointed towards the bank. The landscape was different to the lush and verdant pastures of Byblos. Outside the city, the ground was cracked and hard, the buildings ramshackle and impoverished.

On one small patch on the riverbank, however, a strange mirage had appeared beneath the beating sun. Around it stood a small group of astonished villagers, gazing at each other and then at the trio in the water with a mixture of admiration and fear.

The mirage was a thick sheaf of wheat, sprouting abundantly from a pond-sized bed of compost that his mother would have killed for to grow the Lowmount strawberries.

'Where it had swept up into the village on the tide that Lord Set created, a healthy crop has grown,' said Ice. 'In his footprint, there is food for the poor.'

An elderly man edged towards them. 'Mistress, you must be gods for this is indeed a miracle. Our people have been struggling to feed themselves after selling their meagre crops to support their families. This is enough wheat for every family to have bread for two days.'

'And for the goats to eat well and give of their milk!' cried his wife.

The small crowd joined in eagerly. 'Aye! Aye, a miracle!'

Jack felt terrible for them. 'Two days' worth of bread? It's not much to get excited about, is it?' he muttered out of the corner of his mouth, smiling and nodding at the people on the shore as if he were one of the royal family.

'But this is a miracle of Osiris,' said Ice. 'You must have faith, Little Gold.'

Nephthys prodded him in the shoulder. 'Go. Cut it down and give the villagers their wheat.'

Before he could ask if he was meant to chew it off at the root, Nephthys reached into the deep folds of her gown and withdrew a dagger. It was long and slender, with a simple wooden hilt and a matte grey blade in which Jack could see the indentations of a million hammer-strikes. It was almost as if he could hear the clang of metal on metal; the knife seemed to hum as it lay across the goddess's open palms.

She handed it to him with a smile. 'This is from the Sky Goddess, Nut, who is our mother and grandmother.'

'How is she both your mother and your grandmother?' said Jack with a laugh.

At that, Nephthys's fingers snapped shut over the blade. She moved into towards him in a way that reminded Jack of Seth – stealthy, confident and really quite irritated with him – and for a moment he feared he might feel the dagger slice into his side, burying itself up to the wooden hilt.

Instead of stabbing him, however, the Goddess pulled his hand open and put the dagger in it, wooden shaft first. 'Not our grandmother, Jack,' she whispered. 'Yours. Surely you've worked it out by now.'

Jack gaped at her. 'My grandmother is a goddess who's a nut? No. My *great*-grandmother is Granny Dazzle, and she's a bit mad. Maybe there's some confusion?'

'Only in your small human brain,' said Nephthys sharply. 'Because of the curse, you have two families, Little Gold – a human side and a god side. In this world, Nut of the Sky is my mother and your grandmother.'

'So ... hang on.' Jack stared at her as he tried to work it out. 'Blimey,' he said eventually. 'You're ... I mean, it was hinted at but I didn't really think it was true. Do you mean that you're my ... my other mother?'

Nepthys smiled. 'Your god-mother.'

'That means something very different where I'm from,' said Jack faintly. 'Just someone who comes to your christening and gives you presents on your birthday.'

Nephthys glared at him, wearing the same expression on her face as his mother – his actual mother – when he'd annoyed her. It was an expression he knew pretty well.

'I *was* at your christening, Jack Bootle-Cadogan of Lowmount, though nobody knew it. And I've just given you a present.'

As she spoke, the dagger thrummed gently in his hand, like a gong that had just been struck.

'So you have. It's very nice. Thank you,' said Jack, ever polite - even though he wasn't sure he'd know what to do with a sharp object that sang to itself.

'Geb and Nut preserve us. Just ... go and cut the sheaf down,' she snapped, exasperated. 'Or do I have to do that myself too?'

She was definitely related to him somehow. That was so like his mother – his ACTUAL mother – that Jack had little doubt that she was telling the truth. It was a truth that was both terrible and amazing – rather like his entire existence as a dog-headed young god.

Jack was suddenly filled with a million questions, but Ice was beginning to look very sad over the chunk of foot she held like a baby in her arms. If he didn't move quickly, the villagers' crop would be frozen before they'd had chance to even chomp on the chaff. With a quick backward glance at Nephthys, who he would swear was almost tapping her watch like his mother would do on similar occasions, Jack clawed his way through the low reeds and made his way up the bank, his skin itchy with pins-and-needles wherever the dagger vibrated against it.

'Hello! Sorry, would you like to stand back a bit?' he said to the gaggle of village folk.

'What are you doing?' asked the old man querulously. 'That is our miracle crop!'

'Fear not.' Jack held up a hand and tried to sound godly like his ... like Nephthys and Ice. 'The goddess has ordered me to do this for you.'

Eyeing him suspiciously, the man glanced at the two sisters who still stood knee deep in Nile water, then motioned to the other villagers to stand back.

Jack knelt down at the foot of the sheaf. It was nearly as thick as the trunk of the pillar tree. He stared at the slender blade, wondering if he was meant to saw the wheat down a stalk at a time. This was going to take forever.

But as he gripped the wheatsheaf with his left arm and brought his right hand down towards it with the knife extended, the stalks began to flop easily against his arm. Whining like the tiniest of chainsaws, the dagger sliced effortlessly through the sturdy stalks which seemed simply to melt at the base.

In no time at all, he was scything through the centre of the sheaf. Adjusting his grip so that he didn't slice his own arm off, Jack chopped through the last of the stalks and caught the entire sheaf in the crook of his elbow. It was massive; he needed both arms around it to lift it clear of the ground and hand it over to the village elder.

'There's more there than I thought,' he said.

'A miracle!' whispered the man in awe. Then his eyes widened and filled with tears. 'A true miracle!'

Jack turned to follow his gaze, then burst out laughing. The cropped thicket of wheat was already growing again, green tendrils bursting forth from the sliced stalk ends and the moist ground beneath them, unfurling like streamers thrown at a party until the entire sheaf bristled as high as Jack's head. They all watched in astonishment as the grain ripened to the new golden colour of his hair, then wafted gently against the breeze, ready for harvesting. He should have known better. Even with only one jade foot, Ozzy wouldn't present the village with the means to survive for just a couple of days.

'Like I said,' repeated Jack with a grin. 'There's more there than I thought.'

'And will be forever,' cried Ice who had climbed daintily up the bank, clutching Ozzy's green marble toes. 'Furthermore, to protect it, I will build a temple where the goodness and greatness of Osiris can be remembered always.'

Most of the older people of the village were in tears, overwhelmed by the miracle that had befallen them. 'Please don't trouble yourself, Goddess. We shall build it,' vowed the old man.

Ice smiled at him. 'We shall do it together. Here men and women, gods and mortals are all equal. Together shall we do it.'

And that was precisely how it happened, with the goddesses coaxing the river and the earth into solid foundations and then walls, and Jack and the villagers thatching the roof with the endless supply of stems from the wheatsheaf. When it was completed, the old man donated some clothes to Jack, and he bathed quickly in the Nile before dressing and tucking his new dagger into his belt. Then the whole village celebrated their good fortune with sweet cakes and bread and meat as Ra sank onto the Western bank of the Nile.

As the villagers caroused into the night and Ice sang to them of Ozzy's greatness in her sweet, high voice, Nepthys crouched down beside Jack.

'You have done well, Little Gold. You have kindness in your human heart, and that is every bit as powerful as your god-powers.'

'I think I get that from Granny Dazzle,' said Jack. 'Oh. And you!' he added as an afterthought.

Nephthys laughed. 'It is certainly not from your godfather. You do know who that is, don't you?'

He'd had a horrible feeling about it, of course. 'It's him, isn't it? Seth.'

A frown crinkled the goddess's beautiful face as she nodded. 'It is why he fears you so greatly. Only someone with the same strength of purpose will be able to defeat him. Only you, in other words, Jack Little Gold.'

'I don't think I can do it,' groaned Jack. It all seemed so helpless. 'I keep trying but nothing seems to work. He told me at the river battle that I'd failed, and he was right.'

The goddess nodded towards the dagger that buzzed against his hip. 'But now you have help.'

'Is that why you gave this to me? To defeat him?'

'You've experienced its strength,' said Nephthys. 'If we can combine it with the Pharaoh's Was Sceptre it can make Osiris whole again.'

'And let me guess,' said Jack with a sinking heart. 'The Was Sceptre is that stick that Ozzy was holding, that probably now belongs to someone else.'

'It doesn't belong to Lord Set, Little Gold. It has been stolen.'

'And it's my job to get it back.'

Nephthys nodded, her dark eyes flickering sadly like the candlelight around them.

Jack sighed, scratching the earth with the tip of the dagger. How had this ever even started? It was crazy and just plain wrong. All he'd wanted was to be normal instead of a lord-to-be, and here he was in Ancient Egypt with a mission to do away with the murdering god who was his own father-type thing, apparently. If he ever again saw Albert Cornthwaite and his partner in Egyptian crime, Lord Jay, he'd have more than a few words to say to them. That was where it had all begun – when they found Ozzy's coffin and unleashed the pig-force they knew as Seth. And yet that had been years – decades! – before Jack was even born. How was it possibly fair that he'd been stuck with handling all this?

Then he looked again at what he'd been drawing in the sand. It was a kohl-rimmed eye with flicks at the corner – an eye that had watched him for as long as he could remember, in the comforting shadows of the museum at Lowmount. The eye of Horus, inked by Granny Dazzle or Jay - or maybe even Nephthys herself - onto the door to his home.

He'd been waiting for this, really, for his entire life.

Suddenly, Jack hoisted the dagger back onto his hip and stood up.

'It has been a long day. You are ready to retire?' said Nepthys.

'No way,' said Jack firmly. 'I'm going to find the rest of Ozzy. We're not going to restore him to his throne with just one foot.'

Nephthys smiled with relief. 'Then we accompany you.'

So for hours and days and maybe even weeks without sleep or respite, the three gods roamed the Nile in search of the scattered, shattered remains of Osiris, zipping to wherever a miracle had been proclaimed, building temples to honour them, and gathering jade remnants into a basket of reeds that Jack fashioned using his humming metal dagger. At length, they carried a baker's dozen of Ozzy-pieces around in his reed cradle, but Jack knew it wasn't enough.

There should be fifteen. Fifteen pieces. They were will missing two pieces, including the vital crown which Jack feared would never, ever be found.

Chapter 13

Perched on top of his camel, Albie lurched after Adjo with about as much grace as he'd ever mustered on a horse. In his future past, if there could be such a thing, if had been a source of great amusement and incomprehension to Diselda that he could never sit in a saddle without toppling forward so that his head was directly above the horse's ears. She'd accused him of riding with the skill and flexibility of an ironing board and he'd felt the pain, once again, of disappointing her.

Jay, of course, could ride like Rudolf Valentino in The Sheik, the film that had captured hearts all over the world in 1921. And what he didn't know about thoroughbreds would fit on the twirly ends of his moustache.

Right now, though, Albie didn't care how much cleverer and handsomer and richer and all-round better-at-everything Jay was than his poor apprentice. If they didn't act quickly, Jay would be stupider and every bit as poor as Albie.

'Lord above, he'll lose everything!' he cried in alarm to Adjo.

Adjo cupped an ear as he leaned back on his camel. 'Yes!' he called back amiably.

'Why. Are. You. So. Calm. About. It?' Every word was thumped out of him by the clumsy clump of the camel's hooves. 'He can't. Lose. Everything. I'd never. Forgive. Myself.'

'Ah, sorry! I misheard you. I thought you meant you would lose everything.'

'That's not an improvement!' cried Albie indignantly, but then he thought about it. 'Actually, that is an improvement. I've got nothing to lose anyway. And if I lose spectacularly then Jay will feel vindicated, I hope.'

Adjo's mischievous grin flashed in the sunlight as he waved from this camel. 'Neither of you will lose everything. I have a plan, Master Cornthwaite, never fear!'

'I'm glad one of us does.'

Remembering that some of the camel drivers spoke fairly decent English and might be able to understand them, Albie forced his camel to speed up and see-sawed across the desert after Adjo. He caught him up as they were nearing the city's perimeter and moved in as closely as he dared to without getting a foot bitten off by Adjo's steed, or possibly his own.

'Perhaps you'd better share this plan with me,' he mumbled from beneath his handkerchief as he mopped sweat from his spectacles. 'I'm rather sick of surprises.'

His friend simply grinned again. 'It is preferable that you do not know, Master Cornthwaite. Then you will have – what do they call it on those policeman shows from America on television in our future lives – ah, yes. Plausible deniability!'

'I'll have what?'

'Plausible deniability. You won't know anything because you really won't know anything. And that way you do not have to lie! Which, may I say, Master Cornthwaite, you are really very bad at.'

Albie swallowed nervously. 'Oh Rerek, Adjo. What exactly are you planning?'

But Adjo simply wagged a finger at him. 'No, no! I am telling you nothing. But let us simply say that I have been using my reintroduction to the souk to learn some very useful skills.'

With a wild grin that told Albie far more than he actually wanted to know, the boy hauled the head of his camel towards the city gate and whooped for joy. Albie sighed. Whatever he'd been learning in the bazaar, Albie strongly suspected that it had nothing to do with how to sell moccasins.

Although it was barely two in the afternoon, and the sunshine outside could have cracked Bone's bald pate like a three-minute egg, the atmosphere in the back room of the Oasis Orchid was thicker and darker than dusk in the forest. Wreathes of smoke from hukkah pipes twisted up towards the ceiling, and it was evident from the florid complexions of some of the European gentlemen in the room that the claret had already started to flow.

To his embarrassment, Diselda caught Albie by the wrist as he scrambled through the doorway, close behind

Adjo. 'Mister Cornthwaite ... Albie,' she said hesitantly. 'I'm so sorry to detain you, but I feel we really must talk.'

'We must?' Albie stared at her bleakly. Then he nodded. 'Of course. We must.'

She was of course going to tell him that she loved Jay, and that would be that. His impossible dream would be over. There she was, opening her delightful mouth. Here it comes, thought Albie.

She didn't deliver the words he was expecting, however. 'I can't ... I can't help thinking that you've been avoiding me since I ... since the other night when I rather rashly placed my heart necklace around your neck.'

'Oh!' said Albie, feeling the flush start at his cheekbones and spread to his collar. 'No! Why would I avoid you? Except, yes ... well, perhaps I have.'

Diselda chewed her lip furiously. 'Oh dear. What a pickle I've put us in. You don't want to be associated with me. I quite understand that. I'm a little reckless and racy, I know ...'

'Good lord, no!' shouted Albie. 'That isn't it at all. You're the most adorable person I've ever known and will ever know in my entire life, Diselda Carruthers. I could never be ashamed to be in your presence.'

Diselda's face brightened. 'Really? Because whatever people may think of me, I don't go back on my word, Mister Cornthwaite, and I'm convinced you are similarly forthright. If you and I are somehow betrothed now then I will be honoured – no, not honoured, but quite simply thrilled – to become your ... your ...'

She trailed off, but not because she was repulsed by the idea of becoming his wife, Albie realised. It was because she didn't want to presume that he would want to marry her.

'Believe me, nothing would make me prouder,' he said. And suddenly, Albie knew what he really felt, and what he must really do. 'Apart from this.' He gripped the ends of her fingers. 'The man to whom you should really be betrothed is in that room, about to gamble away his fortune. He loves you utterly, and I'm afraid that if he doesn't find out very soon that you feel the same way, he might implode with misery.'

'But I thought ... I really thought that you loved me too, Albie.'

He placed the locket – her heart on a string – into her palm. 'I love you both. You are my dearest friends in the entire solar system apart from one other person, and actually it's vital that you two get together so that other person can one day step into our worlds – yes, yours too. Oh!' he said, flapping a hand as if the heat were getting to him. 'I'm talking nonsense, but this much is true. All our future happiness depends on you going into that room and placing the locket around Lord Jay Bootle-Cadogan's sweaty neck.'

'I can't!' whispered Diselda.

'He'll be delighted, I assure you!'

Diselda shook her head. 'No, I'm not allowed! No women permitted.'

'Good lord, really?' Albie said, aghast. Things really had changed in the last century.

Then on an impulse, he threw open the door. 'The Diselda I know wouldn't let a little thing like an idiotic rule stop her from doing what she wants. The Diselda I know would grab hold of her heart's desire and her future happiness, no matter what the consequences.'

For a moment she gazed up at him, doe-eyed, and he almost regretted the decision he'd just made. He could tell her it was a joke. Steal away with her like the Sheik in that silent movie. Nobody would need to know, and she wouldn't have to face her fears like this.

But then, to his delight, she laughed aloud and stepped boldly into the room. To the astonishment of all the gentlemen gathered to play poker, and the horror of a good half of them, she slid back a chair, placed a dainty heel on it, and stepped onto the oval table.

In three steps she was across it. With a flourish, she balanced the necklace on the end of her shoe and then draped it around Jay's neck.

'My heart on a string,' she said simply. 'It belongs to you.'

Bewildered, Jay stared at Albie who was still lurking in the doorway. Albie nodded to his friend, and suddenly Jay leapt to his feet and swept Diselda off the table.

'Gentlemen, meet the future Lady Bootle-Cadogan!' he cried.

Several of the men clapped, before one old curmudgeon – Major Farnsworth, whom Albie knew to be particularly fond of port, pastries and poker - rapped on the table. 'There's a game on here, BC,' he barked. 'And even wives of the peerage aren't allowed in this room.'

Jay laughed, unable to take his eyes off Diselda. 'Then I shall leave too,' he said. 'Albie, take my place at the table, will you?'

'And I will play also!' piped a voice from the shadows.

Adjo slid up to the table with the stealth of a cat.

'What the devil—' Farnsworth staggered to his feet. 'Where did that boy come from? No women, and no blasted children!' he bellowed.

'He's ... he's with me,' said Albie quickly as the newly betrothed couple swept past him in search of champagne. He rushed to the table and took Jay's seat, wishing he'd taken more notice during the games his mentor had frequently played. Losing his own hand to placate Jay would have been one thing. Winning to keep Jay's fortune was quite another.

He turned up the corners of Jay's hand, wishing he had the slightest gift for gambling. What Adjo had said was true: he was a terrible liar, and he was fairly sure that his poker face would leave much to be desired. In fact, he was perspiring so heavily in the sub-tropical temperature that the other players could probably see his cards reflected on his forehead.

Three queens, he told himself. That was good, wasn't it? Two black and one red. Okay. And the jack of clubs and an eight of spades. Not so good. But not bad overall. His heart hammering, Albie placed his cards back down on the table and nodded to Major Farnsworth. 'I ... I'll raise you,' he stammered.

The major guffawed. 'How dare you, man? Raise me with what? I don't want your servant boy, and that appears to be all you have to your name. Little more than a servant yourself, from what I can gather, what?'

It was as if a red mist was descending over Albie's spectacles. He shook his head, trying to clear it, but the fog would not disappear. Then he realised that it wasn't mist. It was emotion.

Anger.

'I am not a servant,' he said stiffly, staring the major right between the eyes. He and Jack had faced Seth and all manner of Egyptian monsters, for crying out loud. Did this buffoon think he could intimidate him? 'I am a trained archaeologist, sir, and about to report in an academic paper my significant findings, such as none have ever before witnessed.'

'He is!' cried Adjo, slapping the table jubilantly.

Albie pointed at him. 'And Adjo is nobody's servant either. He is the wisest, oldest soul you could ever hope to know. He has more knowledge in his milk teeth than you seem to have acquired in a lifetime of avoiding active service in His Majesty's army, Major Farnsworthverylittle,' he spat. 'Furthermore, he is a trusted adviser of my very dear friend and my equal, Lord Jay Bootle-Cadogan.'

Farnsworth's face was a riot of colour, but at least none of those hues were green like Seth, thought Albie, on a complete roll by now.

'And so, as I do speak for my friend, Jay, and I am indeed playing his hand for him, I raise you a stable-full of Irish champion thoroughbreds, an ornamental pool of prized carp, and ...' He shoved back his chair, brandishing the cards in the air. '... One. Stately. Home.'

Albie slapped the cards down on the table, face up.

'There!' he roared, hardly able to believe that the voice bouncing off the walls of the Oasis Orchid was his own.

And he looked down at the cards, about to reel off his hand. Three queens, a jack and an eight. He'd overstepped the mark. He was going to lose Lowmount on Jay's behalf.

But then he saw it – the fourth queen. Two blacks, and now two reds. The eight had disappeared.

'Four!' he yelled. 'Four queens and a jack! Beat that if you can, sir!'

He wasn't really sure how it had happened. Perhaps he had been mistaken before. He'd got it wrong; there were two red queens. But then he saw Adjo from the corner of his eye, sidling backwards into the shadows. So that was the skill he'd learned in the souk - sleight of hand! When he'd rapped the table for joy, he must have exchanged the eight for the other red queen.

But then, as he closed up his hand of cards, Albie saw the other red queen.

It was hearts.

There were two Queens of Hearts.

Fortunately, nobody had taken the opportunity to check before Albie had picked them up again, but still, the atmosphere closed in around the table.

Farnsworth hauled his carcass out of his seat. 'This game is over. Tell BC he owes me a re-match. I am not giving up my home on the say-so of an articled clerk.'

'Your hearing must be as bad as your breath, Major,' said Albie. 'I said "archaeologist". And you can settle your debts directly with Lord Jay.'

The major slapped his gloves against his hand, glaring at Albie as if he would very much like to be slapping them repeatedly around Albie's face, neck and shoulders. Then, without another word, he jerked his head at the rest of the players and pushed his way through to the door, quickly followed by the others.

Before his knees gave out, Albie sank back into his seat.

'We won, Adjo! By a …'

'Plausible deniability, Mister Cornthwaite,' murmured Adjo.

Albie swallowed hard. Yes. He wouldn't even say it. If he didn't mention what he'd seen, it would be as if he'd won fair and square. He could take the secret with him to the grave, because it didn't matter any longer. Everything was back on track. Jay and Diselda were together. The Lowmount fortune wasn't lost, and if he could just work out what had happened in the chain of events leading to an empty cave where Osiris should have been, he could correct absolutely everything.

The future-past was suddenly very bright again - for everyone, but especially for him. For Albert Cornthwaite, Archeologist and Academic.

For the first time in as long as he could remember, Albie felt like celebrating.

'Adjo, wasn't Jay talking about champagne?'

'I believe he was!' cried Adjo.

'You do know you can't have any, don't you?'

'Why not?'

'Because you're fourteen.'

Adjo laughed. 'I am fourteen and one hundred, and then some more!'

'Yes, but nobody knows that apart from me. And I suspect it would be best if we kept that information to ourselves.'

'Oh.' Adjo slumped for a second, then resumed with his normal happy demeanour. 'Well, I find it "addles" the brain anyway. All those bubbles in my marbles. I much prefer our honeyed mead. I will go and tell my family of Lord Jay's good fortune while you toast it in here.'

He was just about to exit the room when he turned around again. 'And Master Cornthwaite. Albie. Thank you for your kind words about me.'

Albie smiled. 'I've just discovered that I hate it – being called a servant. Anyone being called a servant. I can't put up with it any longer.'

'Well, I myself do not mind too much because I like being of service to others,' said Adjo, nodding as he thought it through, 'but I see what you mean. Being of service is not the same as being a servant. I will remember that.'

'Exactly. You really are very wise.'

'In my milk teeth.' Adjo displayed all his teeth in a broad grin and then scampered outside. 'I will see you soon, my friend!'

Albie laughed. All these friends. Jay, and now Diselda and obviously Adjo. And Jack. Where was Jack? How was Jack? He was the greatest friend of all of them, and Albie didn't even know where he was. It was probably time to find Minty and see if she could organise some kind of rendezvous for them all. For the longest time he sat in the darkness, wondering about how his life had turned out. When the last candle guttered and extinguished, Albie inhaled deeply, and left the room.

In the front bar room of the Oasis Orchid, Jay and Diselda were staring at each other over the broad, flat rims of their champagne glasses. They looked so deliriously happy that Albie was hesitant to join them, but when Jay saw him he waved him over.

'We're already married!' he said, a trifle blearily, sloshing champagne over the table as he gestured to Diselda. 'The captain of the ship Diselda is booked onto happened to chance by as we ran to the hotel to get the ring, and offered his services! We came back here afterwards to surprise you with the news.'

'Congratulations to you both. I couldn't be happier.' It was a great delight to Albie that he actually meant it. 'And you're not only married, you're rich. Richer, should I say.'

'You sly old thing,' said Jay. 'All this time and I never knew you were a card sharp. Farnworth staggered past as if he were having a coronary.'

'I think he might actually burst,' laughed Diselda.

'I don't actually want his sorry pile of bricks in East Sussex, you know,' declared Jay, 'but it will be nice to have a bit of cash back in the coffers. I'll be able to pay the foreman and his men, and even pay for our passages back home.'

'Ah! Speak of the devil.'

Albie pointed to the doorway where the dig foreman slouched with his usual sulky expression. He was holding a roll of parchment and the box in which he collected the pay for the workers. Behind him, one of the workmen he'd hired rolled his white cap over and over in his hand. Albie grinned to himself. Archeological assistants. That would be his name for them. Not workers or men or even diggers, but trainees on a ladder that would lead somewhere, out of the dig and on to the museums of Cairo and Luxor, to the studies and libraries of the brilliant Fitzwilliam House or King's College, Cambridge or Balliol, Oxford.

The foreman approached, giving Jay a curt nod. 'The major has told me of your winnings. You will be paying us first, I trust?'

'Well, you're a little quick off the mark, but you're absolutely right. As soon as I get some sterling in my hands, I'll pay you and the men. Right before I whisk my new bride back to England and show her around Lowmount.'

But the foreman wasn't prepared to wait. He gripped Jay's flailing wrist in his thick fingers. 'Now, if you please.'

Jay frowned but passed it off with a laugh. 'I don't have it now.'

The other man breathed heavily. Ominously. Albie's guts twisted as he watched the face darken and then look across quickly to the room he himself had just left. The foreman's eyes searched for something, and then he nodded. Albie spun around. The other man, the one with the twisted cap, had just emerged from the games room - only now he wasn't just holding his hat. In his other hand, he clutched a span of playing cards.

Albie's winning hand.

The foreman twisted his fingers into Jay's wrist. 'You have money for champagne and yet you do not pay us. And you win your good fortune by cheating at cards.'

Jay stood up slowly. 'Now look here, I don't know what's bitten you, but I can assure you I have no ready cash, and I certainly – certainly – do not cheat.'

The other man had approached the table, and with a sinking heart Albie realised what he was going to show them.

Four queens, including two Queens of Hearts.

'Jay, let me handle this,' he offered as Jay pushed his face into the foreman's.

'I had nothing to do with that hand,' growled Jay. 'And just to prove it, I'll sign whatever trumped-up deal you have from Farnsworth in your grimy hand, and I'll …' - he plunged his hands into his pockets – 'I'll give you whatever money I have, right this instant.'

Lowering his eyes, the foreman seemed to think about it for a moment, and then he opened the wooden casket ready for Jay's outpouring of guineas and shillings. Jay opened his fist and shoved his fingers in the box, creating a ramp for the coins to slide down.

Something was wrong. Something was circling Albie's thoughts like a wraith, filling his heart with dread.

'Jay, stop—' urged Albie.

But it was too late. Jay cried out, startled, in pain. He withdrew his hand sharply and the casket fell over. Diselda gasped as a scorpion skittered onto the table, poison sac raised to strike again …

Albie tore off his spectacles and used the arm to sweep the scorpion onto the floor where he stamped on it before it could disappear into a corner, and then he reached across to close the wooden box in case there were more in there.

And as he stretched across the table he looked up into the saturnine face of the foreman. For a second, the man looked almost pig-like…

Albie's heart turned over as he realised what he was looking at, and just as he did so the foreman suddenly graced him with a foul and evil smile. With one deliberate wink as Jay slumped to the floor, the man turned and left the Orchid, pausing in the doorway to remind Albie resolutely of the other times he had seen that evil face at close quarters.

Seth.

He had returned.

Chapter 14

Jack looked down at the effigy he'd just laid out on the river bank and sighed.

After finding thirteen chunks of Ozzy scattered far and wide across the countryside bordering the river, and indulging in a great deal of temple-building and partying with the locals, the man-sized green statue was almost complete.

Almost, but not quite.

As far as Jack could tell, they were still missing the left hand and lower arm, and – of course – the crown of Ozzy's head. Even if they found those sections of him, Jack had no idea how they were going to stick it all together and make Osiris whole again. Superglue?

Dawn was rising; in the shallows of the river, the two goddesses were paying their respects to the new day. 'Ra in you, sister,' they proclaimed to each other.

'Ra in you both,' called Jack, quickly jumbling the pieces and placing them back in the reed basket in which he transported them all. It probably wasn't a good idea to let Ice see Ozzy in bits.

Nephthys clearly knew what he'd been up to, though. 'Ra in you, Little Gold. Do we have our travel plans for the day?'

Jack nodded. It wasn't as if he had a map or anything, but being able to focus on the missing sections of Ozzy meant that he could Zip them along to the next location. They'd look for the hand next, but he couldn't prevent the sinking feeling in his gut whenever he thought about the crown. As much as he'd tried to visualise it over the last few days of searching, he could never get a clear image in his mind, and somehow they'd always been transported to a different location and body part. It was as if the wretched crown didn't *want* to be found.

That was more or less what Nephthys had said, too, when he'd asked her about it. 'You cannot find what is lost, Little Gold. Your attention to its lostness keeps it hidden.'

But how could he not focus on its lostness? That was the main thing about the crown – that it had always been missing. Nephthys wouldn't be drawn on the topic any further, however. 'Talking about it more is attention to its lostness.'

'I don't understand.'

'No, because you are looking for the answer to your question and your focus on its absence keeps it at bay. You will find the answer only when you are not looking.'

Jack had tutted. 'My human mother's much more straightforward than you.'

'Sticks and stones, Jack,' Nephthys had replied with an enigmatic smile.

Now she helped Ice with her headdress and washed her hands in the river, not even looking at Jack. Before they set off, the trio ate some of the bread and goat's cheese that the last village had foisted upon them. Jack chewed mournfully, wishing that cows weren't sacred. He was dying for a burger. Or a steak. Even a tin of dog food. He was beginning to miss home, he realised, and not for the first time, he wondered if anyone had noticed he'd gone. For all he knew, Minty could have frozen time at Lowmount. He might return in a week or two to find his mother poised in mid-snip over the agapanthus, or his father in stasis, red in the face from shouting at the newspaper. As for Albie-Bone, Jack couldn't even imagine him at the castle. He'd been dropped off in mid-history somewhere, and Jack didn't even know where. Swallowing the last crust of bread, he sighed again.

'What ails you, Jack?' asked his god-mother.

'Just wondering how everyone is,' he said with an attempt at a smile.

'Missing you, I'm sure.'

'I wouldn't be so sure about that.'

'Oh,' she replied in her low, smooth voice, 'I'm very sure.'

A higher voice chimed in. 'So are we ready to find more of Osiris?'

Ice's thoughts were never far from him. Even when she was helping the Egyptians and Phoenicians to set up their temples and feed themselves from whatever munificence Ozzy had left behind, she was always urging Jack to be ready to move on.

Dusting the crumbs from the robe he'd been given two villages ago (and thanking the stars that Guisely couldn't see him in a dress), Jack got to his feet. 'Yes. We're going to find his lower left arm.' He could picture that with very little effort, having seen it before it was carried away on the crest of a wave.

The goddesses simply nodded and placed themselves in front of Jack with their backs to him, shoulder to shoulder with each other. After a quick transformation to his dog-headed self, Jack clamped an enormous hand around their arm and conjured up a mental image of a green hand and wrist.

The swirl in his stomach signalled the imminent start of their journey. He'd latched onto something, and now his personal sat-nav and auto-drive system would propel them all towards it. 'Please prepare for take-off,' he said in his best pilot's voice, just as he felt the tug from the invisible cord that attached him to whatever he focussed on.

For many miles they Zipped, traversing the river several times as they followed its gentle bends to Ozzy's hand. Jack was concerned to note how this part of their journeying had changed since the flood that Seth had created. Before that, the river had been so wide it was hard to see across it to the other bank; when they zipped through it they were mostly chest deep in water. In recent days, however, the Nile had dwindled to a much narrower channel, exposing the river bed to the sun's harsh rays until it dried and shrivelled into crazy paving. Without Ozzy's whole presence, it was as if the river itself was dying.

Before he could stop to inspect the arid riverbed more closely, they suddenly veered right and swooped up onto the bank. Jack shook his head to rid himself of the image of Ozzy's hand, so that they didn't skid straight up to it and scare any circling villagers half to death. Hidden by the reeds, as Jack let go of Ice and Nephthys so they could steady themselves, he shrunk neatly and instinctively into his Jack form. They looked almost normal as they pushed through the sparse foliage and made their appearance at the latest site of an Ozzy find.

The residents of this particular village – mostly women and female children – were gathered around a dark patch of earth that had appeared at the edge of a field that was otherwise turned to sand. The villagers were mostly too thin and starved to do anything more that stand around it in awe and astonishment.

'Stand back,' said Jack as they approached from the reeds. 'I'll inspect it for you.'

One or two of the children began to scream as the strangers appeared from the river's edge, but Ice hurried forth to place her cool hand on their shoulders. 'This is a gift for you from Osiris, your Pharaoh and god,' she said calmly, as she'd said in thirteen other places. 'Be at peace.'

Nephthys frowned as she looked around her. 'Where are your menfolk?'

'They have been ordered to Luxor to join Pharoah's great army,' said one of the women.

'But your pharaoh, Osiris, does not believe in war,' said Nephthys. 'He would not command this.' She didn't add 'even if he could'. There was a limit to how much information the locals needed to know.

Jack, however, realised exactly what this meant. With a sinking heart, he predicted what the village women was going to say before the words left her mouth.

'Forgive me, mistress, but this is not the word of Osiris. Lord Set is Pharaoh now.'

Before Ice could begin to shake with misery and wrath, Jack placed a hand on her arm. 'We'll find him. All of him,' he whispered. 'Don't give anything away.' To the woman, he said simply, 'Show me what you found.'

Ozzy's left arm was buried almost to the elbow in a fertile little patch a few hundred meters from the Nile's edge – although it would have been on the outer reaches of the river before it started to dry up. Kneeling, Jack dug away some of the earth around the block of jade so that he could get a grip on Ozzy's hand, and was surprised to find his own hands coated in a thick slathering of mud.

'It's completely damp,' he told the goddesses.

'Then it must be a new miracle,' said Ice.

So far they had seen fruit trees feeding swarms of bees and people alike; sheaves of corn, wheat and maize that replenished themselves as soon as they were cut down, and in one village, a reed basket squirming with baby goats, who had run around bleating to the great delight of the children, and the even greater gratitude of the adults who knew what a rich source of meat, milk and skins they would provide.

With a shrug, Jack leaned forward and took a firm grip on the wrist section of Ozzy's marble hand. He withdrew the hand slowly from the ground, and as the wrist and then the back of the hand and the fingers appeared above the surface, a puddle bubbled up in its place. Then, just as the tip of Ozzy's pointing index finger was extracted from the ground, the ground belched rudely and a fountain of sparkling water shot into the air. It cascaded back onto the ground and before Jack's eyes, a hole the diameter of a dustbin fell away into the earth, immediately filling up with water.

'It's like a sink hole,' said Jack, 'or a spring. Or ... hang on a minute – what's that?'

A few curious children joined Jack by the hole as he pointed to the surface. Tiny bubbles were strafing across it, and suddenly the silvery head of a fish popped up into the air, to be joined by another and another until the hole positively boiled with them.

'Nice one, Ozzy,' said Jack under his breath. Then he stood up and addressed the villagers.

'This is your personal miracle,' he explained. 'If it's like all the others, you'll never be able to empty it of fish, or water, come to that. If you set up some sort of irrigation system –' To his astonishment, this came to him from a long-forgotten Geography lesson, which would just prove to his father that his school was decent after all if he ever got back to Lowmount ... '—then you'll be able to grow crops and so on. Probably forever. Yay!'

He stepped away from the spring as fish flung themselves onto the ground, just asking to be eaten, and pointed to a shady spot beneath a tree that had been dying but was now being fed from the roots up. 'We'll build the temple over there, I think, Ice?'

As the rejoicing and temple-raising began, Jack slipped back to the river's edge where he had stashed his Basket of Ozzy among the reeds. There was no point in counting any longer. He knew exactly how many parts there were: fourteen. And he knew that if he pieced Ozzy together like a jigsaw, he would find that all the sections slotted together into an almost perfect statue, but that one piece would still be missing. The same piece that had always been missing, since Ice 'n' Ozzy/Ozzy 'n' Ice had first turned up at Granny Dazzle's funeral and Ozzy had tipped his noggin in Jack's direction. There was a jagged section of Ozzy's head that was open to the elements. His crown.

And it was still gone.

Despondent, Jack hid the basket properly and then trudged back to the newly rejuvenated tree. Several of the children were scrabbling in the earth to create holes for the temple foundations (something which Jack had started insisting upon to ensure the buildings stayed upright if Seth sent further floods or monsoons). Ignoring their cries to join in, Jack stepped behind the tree and sat down. He could almost feel the lifeline of water and sap pulsing through the trunk as he leaned against it, and for a second he recalled another Clearwell lesson – biology this time, about green stuff in plants called chlorophyll made in a process called ... photo-something. He'd look it up when he got back, and then he'd impress his father with the many things he'd obviously been taught properly at the school they'd tried to persuade him to leave.

'If I ever get back,' he muttered crossly.

'First sign of madness, talking to yourself,' said a familiar voice.

It was only then that he noticed a pair of beady eyes peering down at him from the branch above his head. Hathor. That could only mean one thing.

'Minty! Where are you?'

Her face appeared beside the hawk's. 'Right here.'

'Where have you been? Are the others with you? How did you get here? What's been happening?' Wow, once the questions had begun there was no way to stop them. Jack opened his mouth again. 'Why did we get separated? Can I get back home? What are we going to do? Do you know where Ozzy's crown is?'

Minty dropped easily to the ground beside him, her helmet of hair looking ashen and lank.

'Chill!' she said rudely, though for some reason this delighted Jack. She was just so ... so normal! Although with the state of her hair ... and her slightly grey skin ... was Minty ill?

'Sorry. I've just been here on my own for quite a while.'

'But isn't that Ice?' Minty peered around the tree to where Ice was leading a building song. 'And ... Nephthys?'

She glanced at Jack quickly, and in that instant he knew that she was aware of just who Nephthys was to him.

'You could have told me,' he snapped.

She blinked innocently. 'Told you what?'

'All of it,' said Jack. 'Nephthys being my godly mother and him – Seth the Evil Pig and apparently Hippo – is my godly father type person. My grandmother is a nut!'

'She isn't a nut, she's called Nut.' Minty's gaze trailed back to the half-built temple. 'And I didn't tell you because your ... because Nephthys told me and Hathor not to. There's a pecking order, pardon the pun, and I have to do what she says.'

'Well, that's all very –' Jack was about to launch into a complaint as long as the Nile about all the stuff he hadn't been told, but Minty frowned, alarmed. 'What?'

'Where's Ozzy?' she said.

Jack sighed. 'Come with me.'

Out of sight, they slipped down to the reeds where Jack showed Minty exactly where Ozzy was. To his horror, her eyes filled with tears. 'Poor Osiris,' she whispered.

'I'm going to fix it,' said Jack.

Minty slumped down beside the basket. 'I don't think you can. I shouldn't have done it, Jack. I shouldn't have brought you all back. It has messed with Ma'at, the natural order of things.'

'No, seriously, it will all be fine.'

Minty turned on him furiously, and for the first time ever he saw the ancient being that existed beneath the smooth skin of the teenage girl that he knew.

'It won't! Ozzy is dead, and Jay is dying. I, too, am dying. Far from restoring order, you have been here distracting Ice while Ozzy perished, and Albie has been flitting around the pyramids creating the very traumas that started the whole drama in the first place and failing to see what's right under his nose. There's no coffin; no Abydos. He tried to steal Diselda from Jay. Why could he not see the way it's supposed to be? Why? He took the heart on a string – those stupid seeds in a locket! And now he's lost Jay's fortune and caused him to be stung by a scorpion. We haven't put it right. We've made everything worse! Worse than ever! And the earth will suffer, Anubis. The earth will suffer because of us.'

Jack stared at her, terrified, watching her wither before his eyes, decaying like a discarded apple core before blooming briefly again into her teenage persona.

What had they done?

'I don't know what to do,' he said simply, looking around for Nephthys. She was always calm. She could advise him.

Instead of the goddess, his eyes fell upon the watering hole and the tree adjacent to it. An idea occurred to him, and he grabbed Minty's hand in a way he would never have dared to do if she was at full strength. Or maybe he would. Whatever he had to do to save a friend, he knew he would try it.

'Come with me,' he cried, half-carrying, half-dragging her towards the spring. 'There. Drink.'

He scooped up water with his bare hands and poured it into Minty's mouth, and then he propped her up against the tree and ran back for more, practically throwing it at her. He'd be in the most enormous trouble if she revived. When. When she revived.

To his relief, she held up a finger as he approached with both hands filled with water.

'Just you try it,' she said bitterly.

Jack laughed. 'You're feeling better!'

'No, I'm feeling wetter.' She pawed at her dripping hair. 'I might have to kill you.'

'Oh, you're definitely on the mend,' said Jack, watching her as she lay back against the comforting solidity of the tree trunk with her eyes closed. 'Watch it, though. If this was Ozzy's tree, the trunk would open up and swallow you just about now.'

Minty sat up quickly. 'Thanks for the warning,' she said, easing herself away from the tree.

The tree.

Jack's heart stopped as he stared at Minty, leaning against the trunk.

It was just as Nephthys had promised. Suddenly, while he wasn't looking for it, Jack got the answer he'd been seeking.

'I know where it is,' he hissed, hardly able to believe it himself.

All this time. All this time looking for something that was missing, when it wasn't missing at all.

He hauled Minty to her feet. 'I know where Ozzy's crown is. We have to go. Now! And collect Albie and Adjo on the way if we can.'

'I don't have the powers,' said Minty. 'Look how I messed it up on the way here, sending you to two different locations and times. It's taken everything I've got to leave 1922 and find you here. I'm sorry, Jack.' She peered at him from under her fringe, which no longer shone with its usual ebony gleam. 'I can't correct all of that.'

'Please!' cried Jack, just a little desperately. 'You have to try!'

Minty shook her head. 'I'd only make it worse, just as Albie is doing at the Oasis Orchid.' Once again, her eyes filled with tears, which was almost more shocking to Jack than her slightly inhuman appearance. Ancient gods he could deal with. Minty being a bit girly – that was just plain wrong. But there was no doubting her conviction that she couldn't help. 'My control over time and space is too limited,' she continued. 'There's just no way I can do it.'

'But there is another way,' announced a voice behind them.

Nephthys had appeared like a ghost beside the tree and had evidently heard every word.

'Ah!' Jack cried. 'You have those powers!'

'No, that is beyond even me, I'm afraid. I can shift through time or space, but not both at once, and not with multiple bodies to transport at the same time.' She smiled mysteriously, in the way that Jack had discovered usually meant there was some riddle for him to work out. 'But your grandmother, Little Gold – she is the one you need for this.'

'Granny Dazzle is—' Jack started, and then he realised who Nephthys was referring to. 'You mean Grandma Nut.'

His god-mother nodded serenely.

'Okay! Take me to her and let's get on with this.'

But of course, he realised, it wasn't going to be that straightforward, because nothing with Nephthys ever was. She was always testing him, trying him out, goading him into action and devising ways to make him work things out for himself.

Nephthys pointed to the dagger in Jack's belt. 'You have the means already, Little Gold.'

'Yeah, meant to say, what's with the hair?' hissed Minty.

Jack ignored her. 'The dagger?'

'You must combine it with the Was Sceptre to create the Phoenix Wand in order to meet with the great Sky Goddess.' Nephthys was talking in riddles again. 'Bring the basket. We must go now.'

'Where?' said Jack and Minty together.

The goddess was already running towards her sister, gesturing to her to leave the temple, to come with them. She turned back before the villagers could hear her.

'To Pharaoh's Palace.'

Jack felt a little faint as he suddenly recalled where he'd seen the Was Sceptre. 'It's Pharaoh's stick thing, and with Ozzy in pieces, the Pharaoh is now someone we're not very fond of,' he muttered to Minty.

'Rather you than me,' said Minty grimly.

But there was no time to discuss it further, because already the goddesses were dragging their barque to the river's edge. The gritty, slimy riverbed disappeared as Jack ran towards it, supporting a much-weakened Minty. They scrambled onto the barque just as it was submerged beneath the great surge of water that Nephthys had summoned. His arms whirled around as his lungs filled with dank liquid, pulling him further into the new depths of the Nile. Minty's fingertips were just beyond reach, and in the pitch darkness he couldn't make her out any longer. His nostrils, throat, ears all burned as though acid were being poured into them, but even worse was the pain from the vice-like jaws gripping his ankles, ready to spin him over and over at the bottom of the river until he drowned or the crocodiles just ate them alive …

But suddenly he worked out that it was a hand that was clamped around his leg, holding onto him, turning him upright, dragging him onto the barque. Coughing up gallons of inky water, Jack dared to open his eyes and found himself lying beside Minty who was in a similar state. Over the pair of them loomed Ice, checking them over with medical precision. 'They live,' she called to her sister, 'and so must Osiris!'

'By Geb and Nut,' cried Nephthys, 'River, carry us!'

A powerful current carried them forward. They were all afloat, whisking along the Nile at speeds that no amount of Zipping could ever achieve. In moments, they would arrive back at the very point where Ozzy had first disappeared in Seth's suffocating wooden coffin.

It was the final battle. He could feel it. To merge the dagger and the Was Sceptre he must defeat the person who held it, and Jack knew beyond all doubt that it – the end of Seth – was all down to him.

Chapter 15

It was like Zipping on a whole new scale, as if they were plummeting down a log flume at the speed of sound. Jack was pretty sure he heard a sonic boom somewhere along the way as they passed through the sound barrier. Nephthys might not be able to cover time and space in one go, but she was pretty impressive at supersonic Nile travel.

With a mighty swoop, the wave that had carried them from the distant realms of the land rushed towards Pharaoh's palace and delivered the barque to the prettily decorated jetty. It was the difference, Jack recognised, between Zipping to a place that was purely imaginary and heading for somewhere that you knew at close quarters. This was Nephthys' home, so they were able to glide to an elegant stop at the perfect point rather than ploughing through the reeds and bursting into the palace through a wall, as he was sure they would have done had he been in the driving seat. He peered sneakily at Nephthys as they all disembarked. While he didn't really want to know how he could be the son of two different sets of parents, he could at least understand that he got certain traits from each of them. The brilliant zip-travel thing – well, that was definitely inherited from his god-mother.

'We had better prepare ourselves.' Ice dusted down her gown where the hem had trailed in the sand of many a temple. 'With providence, Lord Set will not be expecting us, but his power is vast and terrible.'

'Terrible and vast it is,' agreed Jack, very relieved to see a second vessel arriving behind theirs, loaded with Wepsit and his small army of falcon-headed soldiers. 'But we can't let the thought of it stop us.' He was telling himself more than anything. The thought of it could quite easily stop him if he pondered on it for too long. The best thing to do in these circumstances, especially where Seth was concerned, was to take a deep breath and plunge in. 'Come on,' he continued, transforming into his Anubis guise as he ran. 'Let's go see what he's up to.'

They entered the enormous hall of the palace behind the dais where the four thrones of the kings and queens of Ancient Egypt had been lined up when Jack first arrived. Jack heard Ice draw in a sharp breath and immediately understood why.

There was only one throne on the platform. The others lay smashed into splinters around it. It was clearly a message for the Ice, Nephthys and Ozzy. There was no longer a place for them in ruling of the kingdom ... a kingdom that had changed beyond recognition.

Gone was the joyful, fun-filled atmosphere of the party they had left behind. In its place was a brooding and sinister cloud, an atmosphere of forced jollity so brittle that at any moment the hordes of people dancing and carousing could run from the palace in terror, or turn on any strangers to rip them limb from limb.

Seth was not lounging in the remaining throne. Instead, he was using a large stretch of the cavernous room for an indoor archery session, aiming arrows haphazardly at the line of servants who had been tied to a row of scaffolds. Each held above his head an object that Seth was meant to be aiming at – a golden ewer, a faience bowl, a pewter platter – and though it was not clear from the number of bleeding, wounded scalps and forearms whether Seth was a bad shot or he was deliberately missing the targets, Jack was pretty sure he could hazard a good guess.

Nepthys was the first to cry out. 'Lord Set! Stop your cruel games.'

Seth spun around, his fleshy features sharpening as he cast his eye across them all. Jack was suddenly reminded of the various forms he had taken – a thin, sneering boy in Gouldian Finch; a fleshy female secretary whose soft appearance masked a chilling truth; a pig-faced monster. In every case the same glittering eyes had lasered into him as they did now, and even with the support of two powerful goddesses and a legion of mythical soldiers, Jack felt incredibly afraid - not just for himself, but for the tied-up servants, the other rulers of Egypt, for Ozzy and Albie and Minty, and for Ma'at, the natural order of all life which Seth threatened at every turn.

He had to take action, immediately and decisively. He could not leave Seth in a position where he could exert his power any longer.

And to do that, he would need to get hold of the Was Sceptre.

Of course, Seth had it close beside him, held by two of the scorpion women, their tails poised ready to lash out at anyone who came near. It looked like such a simple staff – long and simply carved as if it had very recently been merely the branch of a tree, with a forked bottom that seemed to anchor it to the floor. At its top was an animal head. From this distance it was hard to see what creature it was, but Jack was fairly certain that it was no longer the elongated feline head that Osiris had carried. This was broader and bigger, blunt-featured and ponderously powerful. A pig? Seth could obviously change that head as often as his own.

'Sisters,' he whispered to the goddesses, 'how am I supposed to get to the Was Sceptre?'

Beside him, Ice was shaking from head to toe. 'Traitors! Those scorpions are my protectors. How can they have turned against us?'

'I wouldn't be so sure that they have. Seth might not have given them a choice,' said Jack. 'See if you've still got any power over them and try to draw them off, and then I'll grab the Sceptre.'

Ice and Nephthys nodded together, then waved to Wepsit and the soldiers who instantly lined up behind them in two platoons. Headed by a goddess, the squadrons then separated to skirt the hall, out of the reach of Seth and his minions until they could close in like the pincers of the very scorpions they were attacking. Around them the people encircling the hall, cooking or dancing or serving food, flung themselves aside with expressions of terror on their faces that reinforced Jack's first impression. They were here at Seth's command, probably on pain of death, so that they no longer knew whether to hide from Seth's enemies or defend him from them.

Echoing in the cathedral heights of the palace ballroom, Ice's terrible cries suddenly burst against Jack's eardrums. 'Petet and Tjetet, I name you! Do you follow me or Lord Set?'

Seth raised his bow immediately and released a volley of arrows in Ice's direction. 'Kill them, as ordered,' he said coldly.

The two scorpion women turned, confused, and Jack took the opportunity to race straight towards them and slide beneath a quivering tail towards the sceptre. Sensing his presence, the first scorpion lashed down with her poison sac; it crashed against the floor beside Jack's head and he ducked to one side, thrashing out with his legs so that they became entangled in the scorpion woman's scuttling pincers. She fell to the floor beside him, trying to lance at him with her sting. Jack pivoted on his side and pushed against her body with his feet, narrowly avoiding contact with the venom sac as he shoved the first woman into the second. They collided and clattered to the ground, their armour-plated legs ringing like iron on iron as their legs meshed in the confusion.

'Don't let him control you,' he yelled as the women careened into each other.

They were both scrambling for purchase on the marble floor, trying to right themselves as they aimed their stingers at him. In their confusion, the sceptre clattered to the floor, bridging the gap between the two arachnids and their new leader. Seth saw it fall and was instantly in motion, running towards it as he mutated, horribly, deliberately.

Ice and Nephthys were suddenly beside Jack, the two goddess-led squadrons raising their weapons and screeching like the birds of prey they were as they closed in on the scorpions.

'Go easy on them, Ice,' cried Jack. 'I don't think they know what they're doing.'

'Easy I will go,' replied Ice with a wink. She removed her pronged headdress and held it out before her, a twin dagger to stab through both women at once if the moment required it.

The women lunged for her, but Nephthys called out behind them. They spun around, confused, as Ice then yelled out their names. 'Petet and Thejtet! Who do you follow?'

'Lord Set,' said the first scorpion woman, her hair blazing red.

The other woman hesitated. 'Goddess, I follow … Lord Set is our leader, and yet …'

'Drop your tail, Petet,' cried Ice. 'We have no quarrel. You have been manipulated.'

The woman shook her head, the venomous tail drooping. 'Yes, you are right, Goddess. We have no quarrel.'

But to Jack's horror, the other woman was still on the attack, her hair and the back of her gleaming scales burnished with a deep scarlet light like the rivulets of blood flowing down the arms of the servants that Seth had been using for target practice. Straddling him with all eight of her clicking, terrible feet, she pinned him by the neck with one of her pincers. In her eyes was the same dazed expression of the other scorpion woman, but overlaying the cloud of doubt was a sharp, angular focus, the like of which Jack had only ever seen in one set of eyes: Seth.

He chanced a look around him. Seth was making his way towards them but was severely hampered by Nephthys and her team of falcon-heads. The goddess tripped and tangled Seth with reeds that wound around and around his legs and torso, only to be chopped away by the servants protecting Seth against their own will and wisdom. Meanwhile the soldiers tried to corral the man with their spears, prodding him at intervals to propel him towards the cells where Jack had been held.

The sceptre lay between them. At the same moment, both Jack and Seth started towards it. It was obviously an artefact of great power – the power to rule over all of Egypt – but Jack had a rumbling in his gut that told him there was more to it than perhaps even Seth knew. He had to get hold of it somehow. Before Seth.

'I'm really sorry,' he told the scorpion woman leaning over him.

He lashed out with his dagger; it glanced off the creature's shell as if it really were armour, but the fact that it didn't damage her in any way didn't seem to matter. He'd had the desired effect. The woman was so startled that she instantly reared up to coil her tail around for her attack, and in the surprise she let go of his neck. Jack pictured the Was Sceptre in his mind's eye and instantly began to slither towards it, half-in and half-out of the marble flooring so that it rose like a mountain range around him, splintering with the deafening cracks of a disintegrating iceberg.

He was nearly there. The forked bottom end of the Was Sceptre was just millimetres away from his face. If his arms weren't trapped beneath the marble, he'd have had hold of it immediately. Instead he had to pause, righting himself, tearing his body out of the ground like a mummy slicing itself free of its sarcophagus – and suddenly Jack recalled how this had all started. With Albie. With Granny Dazzle. With Will Waite and mummification.

And with Seth.

His fingers stretched towards the Was Sceptre. Time to end it now. Around him the cries of goddesses and mythological creatures in battle assaulted his ears, but Jack calmed himself enough to gather his strength for the task ahead and reached out for the crook, just as a hideous blood-red foot, clawed and wizened and vast, stamped down on his hand.

Jack screamed in agony and lifted his head, his heart sinking. A gigantic body blocked out the sunlight, and he could suddenly see why the scorpion's back had glistened like an open wound. Seth had fought off Nephthys and exchanged his puny human body for that of a creature of the Nile – a hippo as scarred and battered as a warhorse, as powerful and sinuous as an alligator, and with a stench like an open sewer.

'Seth,' he gasped, trying not to breathe in the smell, 'aren't hippos a bit – you know – cuddly?'

The hippopotamus ground down with its foot. 'So many facts of which you are unaware, BC,' snarled the familiar supercilious voice. 'They kill more humans than any other animal. They are aggressive, excessively so when protecting what is theirs. And they have sharp teeth.'

'I'm pretty sure they're vegetarians, though,' whispered Jack through his pain as the enormous beast stamped its entire three tonne body weight down onto his wrist. Without his Anubis form, he would have died of the pain. Even with it, he doubted he'd ever play basketball again.

The creature laughed. 'I don't want to eat you, Dog-headed one. Merely to render you dead and end your constant interference with my plans. You and your undertaker friend – you have been the greatest obstacle to my greatness. Dealing with Osiris was child's play compared with getting shot of you two.'

'But you haven't yet,' hissed Jack faintly.

He didn't have to pretend to sound as if he was close to passing out. The agonising pain was emanating in waves down his body. However, the more Seth believed he was winning, the more advantage Jack would have in the end ...

... the advantage that came from talking about Albie and Ozzy as if they were already dead, for instance, which proved that Seth had severely underestimated them all.

Or the advantage of having one arm still buried beneath the marble floor of the hall.

An arm that was holding a dagger.

Almost afraid to close his eyes in case he fainted, Jack's eyelids fluttered as the strain of trying to concentrate overtook him. Seth laughed triumphantly, convinced that the end had come for his nemeses.

And in the second that Seth threw back his gigantic, scarred head, Jack drew his arm up through the ground and Zipped towards the Pharaoh's crook. Seth roared as the humming metal dagger ripped through his flesh like a scythe, slicing off the foot that had pinned down Jack's other arm so that the monstrous creature overbalanced, slumping to one side like an overturned tank.

Jack's dagger slid into the forked crevice of the Was Sceptre, vibrating so vigorously that it was all he could do to hang onto it. The hilt of the dagger split in his hand; he gripped it as hard as he could, still lying on the floor – no, still half-submerged *in* the floor – and lifted the newly created instrument towards the ceiling. The bottom third was his dagger, and the top two thirds were the Was Sceptre, but together they seemed form some kind of lightning rod. What had Nephthys called it? The Phoenix Wand or something equally magical…

Because there was no doubt at all that it was magical. Unable to help himself, Jack was dragged through the marble to his feet by the sheer power of the blinding beam of light emanating from the crook. The vibration juddered through him, shaking him from the tips of his ears to his toes as if his cells were rearranging themselves. Suddenly the light spread out above his head, spanning out in ever increasing circles – no, not circles, but hexagons – until all that Jack could see above him was a vast, pulsating dome of light, and through the centre of it, the night sky alight with stars. Around the edge of the dome was a diamond-white hexagon of what he could only describe as solidified starlight, resting at a forty-five-degree angle about a hundred metres up in the air. It rotated gently, humming with the same intensity as his dagger, though amplified by about a million. The whole image reminded Jack of something. Not a rocket, but something like it.

Then he remembered. 'It's like a space station,' he said.

Before he could even turn his brain to asking Nephthys what was supposed to happen next, the sceptre flew upwards, catapulting Jack through the centre of the dome of light and into a star-spangled night sky that simply swallowed him up, until all he could see was blackness and white.

Darkness and light.
Dark and light.
Dark.

Chapter 16

'Welcome,' said a silvery voice that seemed to speak through him rather than to him.

Jack opened his eyes gingerly. It felt as if his eyeballs had been turned inside out by whatever incredible journey he had just made. Assuming he had just made it. He could have been unconscious for days. Weeks. He might even be dead, seeing as it was incredibly bright around him and whoever had spoken to him sounded ... well, angelic.

He blinked against the light that filtered between his eyelashes. Above him, a face gazed down at him with the kind of tenderness that Jack had only ever seen in Granny Dazzle's expression. He blinked again, just to be sure that what he'd seen was correct.

Not the expression. That was definitely very sweet and gentle.

The face. That was the strange thing. It was very long with a pointed chin, a small, lipless mouth and vast eyes that burned with the same intensity as Seth's - although these eyes were kind and velvety black, like a midnight sky. The face stood proud of a crop of illuminated hair that stood straight upright, like electrical cabling that had been sawn off part-way, and was very high up. Whoever was speaking to him had to be three or four metres tall.

He coughed up a few chunks of marble, and a long, tapered hand patted him on the shoulder. He stopped coughing instantly.

'Ah, good,' said the small mouth. 'Better out than in.'

Opening his eyes completely, Jack took in the creature before him. It was indeed several metres tall, with skin that gleamed like stars so it was impossible to see where its clothes began and its body ended, apart from the eye-apertures in its face that seemed to be like windows onto the Milky Way. It was beaming down at him with that exquisite curiosity and tenderness that he'd thought he'd seen before, inspecting him beneath a lantern of starlight that should have seared his eyeballs but somehow did not.

'Are you an … an angel?'

The voice tinkled with laughter. 'No, dear child. I am your grandmother.'

Granny Dazzle was even more dazzly than usual, thought Jack. And she was taller – about four times as tall – and seemed to have lost some facial features and a lot of human hair.

'Come, Anubis,' chimed the woman. 'With great pleasure I show you my home. I anticipate this moment across galaxies.' She waved a celestial arm and Jack found himself on his feet.

And then Jack realised his mistake.

This was his other grandmother. His godly grandmother.

'You're my Nut, I mean, my grandmother, Nut. The Sky Goddess.'

The woman-creature said nothing, but simply folded her hands together and tipped her head to one side. Then, as she opened and closed her enormous eye-holes, Jack felt rather than heard her voice.

'I am. And you are the progeny of Nephthys. Glad am I to meet you. Heart-glad,' she said, somehow into his own heart, with the same vibrating quality to her voice as the metallic hum of Jack's dagger. 'And there is more,' she continued suddenly, angling her head still further as if she were listening to something in the distance. 'You have earthly parents too.'

'Err, yes,' said Jack.

'Then you are indeed the most special and fortunate of progeny.'

Jack snorted. 'I'm not sure I'd call it fortunate. I'm think I'm just weird in both families.'

'And weird is bad?' Nut's voice reverberated around his chest cavity - he felt as though he could hear it in his ribs. 'Surely it is just your unique nature, which is something to be cherished and encouraged, that you call weird?'

'I can tell Nephthys is your daughter,' said Jack. 'She likes talking in riddles too.'

'It is only a riddle until you have worked out the answer. Then it is self-evident.'

'Like how you can't find what's lost if you focus on its lostness.'

'Exactly like that.'

It was only while he was considering this that Jack realised he'd been drifting along beside Nut without moving his feet. He looked down and it was exactly as he'd thought: the ground and his feet were about half a metre apart, and his ... Nut ... seemed to be dragging him along on a buoyant wave of niceness that glowed out of her like white smoke. He looked back at where he'd come from, and all his breath left him in one mighty outburst.

'Noooo!'

Nut gazed back at what he'd just seen. 'You believe you are still on your Earth?'

'I ... didn't really think at all,' said Jack. 'But then, I couldn't ever have thought of this.'

They seemed to have travelled a vast distance in the few short moments since he opened his eyes. The vista rolled away from him like the view from the top of a mountain. On a very clear day. On the moon.

Except that it wasn't the moon. Far beneath him, Jack could see a familiar globe drifting in its orbit, and the Earth's moon bobbled like a pebble in the ocean beside it. He was on a different planet entirely, perhaps even in a different universe, judging by the ripples and waves of stardust that waxed and waned around him like the tide of a circular sea. In the distance across the undulating landscape of Nut's home, the hexagon of starlight twinkled and pulsed. So that was how he'd got her. It *was* like a space station. An actual travel-through-space station.

But then what lay between the space station and where they stood – or hovered - was a series of objects and scenes that were both entirely familiar and completely extraordinary to Jack. A network of broad avenues spanned out in a hexagonal shape that reflected the space station, carved from stark white dust that could have shimmied down from the starlight around them. Each avenue was guarded by a pair of vast statues, sunken into the sandy surface to display a row of human faces crowning cat-like bodies. 'Human heads, lions' bodies,' muttered Jack. 'They're sphinxes!'

And then he saw what the avenues led to. On the shimmering, ice-bright horizon at the end of each of the wide pathways stood a building - a lone building, each one pointing towards its own individual constellation of stars, whose light could flood into them through the small apertures in their tips. Enormous buildings made up of four triangular sides, topped off by a glowing golden helmet. What had Albie called them? A capstone.

'What are they?' said Jack hoarsely, raising a trembling hand in their direction.

Nut laughed gently. 'Those are our homes, Jackanubis, my lovely boy.'

'No. Well, they might be, but they're also pyramids.'

The woman of light inclined her head gracefully. 'I believe that is what you call them on Earth.'

'So ...' Jack wished Albie was there too. He'd be bursting with questions like Jack was, but he'd know what order to ask them in. He'd ask questions that people wanted to know the answers to on Earth, like – how did they build them? What were they for? 'How did you build them? What are they for?' he blurted. 'Oh, and why does my dagger hum?'

Nut motioned to him to sit down, although she herself simply remained in mid-drift, an angelic fork of lightning, and something else that he didn't really want to name that started with A followed by an L and an I and an E and ending with an N.

'They are only riddles until you know the answer, and then it is self-evident,' she repeated. 'Do you not have control over matter, grandson?'

'Well, I can Zip through cars and marble and stuff, but ...' Jack thought about it for a moment. 'Yes, I suppose I do.'

'Then that is how we build them. And do you not have a tall building to call home, my child?'

'Well, I live in a castle, which is a very tall building, but not everyone does.'

'Not everyone is you.'

'So why does my dagger hum?' Jack shouted triumphantly. He'd catch her out on this one. 'Because I don't own any other vibrating knives, no matter who or what I am.'

Nut's black eyeholes narrowed and opened again. He had the feeling she was smiling.

'It hums because it is singing out to where it comes from. Does it sing now?' The tapered fingers pointed to his belt. 'You have it on you.'

Jack glanced down, surprised to find that it was there. Normally he knew of its presence because of the pins-and-needles sensation it gave out, but now it lay completely still and silent. 'It ... it comes from here?'

'It is formed from our star crystals. Meteorite, I believe you may call it.'

'Wow,' said Jack. 'Wowwwwww.' He huffed gently. 'That is a lot to take in. It's going to take me a while, I think.'

The alien woman who appeared to be his grandma simply hovered over him, completely unruffled. 'As while as you need,' she said mysteriously, 'for there is no time construct here.'

So now that was something else he was going to have to absorb. 'There's no time construct?' What did that mean, exactly? 'Wait. There's no such thing as time?'

'There's no such thing as "wait",' said Nut, 'for that is to do with time. There is only now. I speak always in the now, and live always in the now.'

'And ...' The question was going to sound weird. 'Where is now?'

'You are on the Dogstar, Sirius, the brightest star in the sky. This touches you as you travel with the winds, dear greatness.'

'Is that why my hair turned this colour?' cried Jack, clutching his head.

A laugh tinkled around between his ears. 'When you are touched by stars, you shine as bright – and for you, it is in your beingness. Sirius rises bright in the sky in the season of Ahket, the Inundation. The time of Osiris. Our people of Egypt seek it out to tell them the flood is coming, and the fertile land and the goodness of all nature. It is also imbued with the knowledge of the four Galilean moons and the geometrical rings of Saturn. With such glories and endless time are you blessed, Jackanubuis. '

With his brain stretching to overload, Jack stared at her, trying to work it all out. It was important, what she'd just said, but he couldn't quite work out why. He felt some kind of anxiety in his chest, but then when he realised that time didn't matter, it eased and disintegrated into nothingness. If there was no such thing as time, he could take as much *while* as he needed to work it all out. And maybe if there was no such thing as time, there was no such thing as space here, either. Maybe that was why he could move through solid matter. It didn't really exist in this world, a world with which he was somehow connected.

He liked this world, too. It was peaceful. He could take all the while he could ever want, figuring it all out, counting the stars, visiting other galaxies through the hexagonal portal thing which he decided to call the starfield, as it was probably up to him.

And it was just as he was contemplating all of this peacefulness that the memory came to him. Behind him, he had left a complete lack of peace. He had left Seth with a severed foot, furious and possibly not dead. He had left Albie and Adjo in 1922, trapped in a loop of horrific mistakes that would torment them both for eternity. And he had left Ozzy in pieces, still missing his crown, still unable to restore Ma'at to an ancient world which had somehow wrapped him – Jack Bootle-Cadogan of Lowmount – in its wrinkles and folds.

Of course.

It was why he had come here. Suddenly time seemed very important indeed.

'I need to go back,' he said quickly. 'I came here to find you because you're the only one who can take me through both time and space and whatever else I need to cross.'

The elongated head nodded as the cut-off electrical cabling at the back of her head suddenly grew and grew, weaving beautifully across the starlit sky like a network of glow-worms that reached out and connected with the surface of the Dogstar. 'And so it is now,' said Nut. 'Go with love to wherever and whenever you need. I am here to help.'

Suddenly he wanted to hug her. Well, she was his grandma, after all – even if she was unusual.

'Glad I am to meet you,' he stuttered, trying to emulate her strange way of speaking.

The vast pools of ebony darkness blinked. 'And I you, beloved. Always here in your now.'

For a second she held up her lantern. It reflected in the jet-black apertures of her eyes, and suddenly she blinked. Two miniature lanterns beamed out in front of her like a cinema projection, crossing the starlit sky to meet in the centre before the laser of light sent one flying into his chest. His own lantern – right there inside him. She would always be with him. He understood that, somehow, deep in the marrow of his bones and the thump of his heart. He could call on her whenever he needed her because she would always be in his 'now'. It was very, very comforting, especially given that he was about to try and save another of her children: the great god and pharaoh, Osiris.

'Please take me to Ozzy's crown,' he said simply. 'And can I collect Albie and Adjo on the way? Oh, and Minty! And Ice and Nephthys, and anyone else I've forgotten.'

The great tall figure spread her arms wide and sang out a note that echoed in his heart, filling him with a feeling of such power and joy that Jack almost wanted to laugh.

'It is so,' she said gently, and he felt a hand fashioned from starlight pass lightly across his hair.

He opened his eyes again, and he was there, and there once more.

Chapter 17

'Lord above, Jay,' hissed Albie furiously. 'How have we managed to find ourselves here again?'

Unfortunately, Jay was unable to answer him, owing to his having died a few hours earlier.

It was a terrible, horrifying, jaundiced instance of déjà vu. Albie could hardly believe his ill luck. He hadn't managed to prevent a single one of the awful things that had occurred in 1922 from happening. He and Jay had still fallen out. Diselda still loved Jay and not him. And Jay – 'Damnation, man!' screamed Albie in the deepest of frustration – had still died from the venom of a scorpion sting, murdered because he had cheated at cards in a poker game, holding two Queens of Hearts in his winning hand.

Except that - 'Double damnation, man!' hollered Albie, at himself this time – it wasn't exactly as it had all happened before. On this second run at it, Albie had managed somehow to get himself even more embroiled and culpable. He had broken Jay's heart by daring to think that Diselda the Dancing Darling might love him, Albert Cornthwaite, in the same way as she adored Lord Jay Bootle-Cadogan. He had utterly failed to find the resting place of Osiris and create fame and fortune for them all – in fact, it was as if the resting place they'd discovered previously had never existed.

And worst of all – 'Damn and blast it. Do you hear me, Ra? Damn and blast it all!' raged Albie at the skies – it wasn't Jay who had cheated at cards. It was Albie. Unwittingly, Albie had created the very situation which had led to Jay's demise, at the hands of the pig-faced god who would doubtless be appearing to Albie at any moment, taunting him for his ineptitude and guilt. It was his fault that Jay had died. He might as well have murdered his friend himself. First of all, he'd shredded the poor man's heart and reputation into tatters and then he'd finished it off with the sting to end all stings. It was all such a damnable mess and there was nothing he could do to put it right.

Apart from this one thing. It was the thing he had done before. The thing that had appeared to protect Jay's spirit and Diselda's well-being and had turned Albie into an immortally mute bald butler – that thing he could do again. He would do again. He must do again.

Even if the mere prospect of it terrified him.

'What?' he barked suddenly. 'What are you staring at?'

Adjo leaned against the wall of the cave, watching with interest as Albie paced the floor and ranted at intervals. 'I am staring at you, my friend,' he said simply. 'It appears you may be taking leave of your senses.'

'Oh no. I did that long ago. Long, long, long ago.' He pointed to the body that ran like an exclamation mark down the centre of the cave, stretched out on the trestle table they'd purloined from the foreman's tent. 'The last time I did this was when I truly began to lose my marbles, Adjo. I can only imagine it'll be worse when I take a second pass at it. There's less brain to befuddle, for one thing. What little I have left could probably be annihilated with one nasty green breath of Seth when he pokes his piggy little face through the wall. Because it took place in this very cave, you know, where I should have found Ozzy's coffin.'

Spreading his hands wide, Adjo allowed himself a little frown. 'You are too hard on yourself, Master Cornthwaite. All you have been trying to do is put things right. It's not your fault if love and so on are in the way. Not entirely, anyway.'

'Thanks,' said Albie bleakly. 'That helps a lot.'

He willed his friend to shut up so he could concentrate, but it seemed that Adjo hadn't finished doling out advice. 'And,' he declared, holding up a finger as if testing the wind, 'there is no evidence to suggest that just because something went badly before, it will go as badly again.'

'I don't believe it will go as badly, Adjo. I believe it will be even worse. Just like everything else.'

'Well,' said Adjo solemnly, 'there is only one way to find out. And this time it is different, because I am here too.'

Albie dared to brighten, if only a little. 'That's true. I was on my own last time. Dragging Jay's body here was nigh on impossible on my own. It was much easier with you to hold the other end of the table like a stretcher.'

'There you are. And did we meet any difficulty extracting him from the Major's musky cellar?'

'No.'

Actually, it had gone quite well, and largely because Adjo had proved quite ingenious at inventing methods for transporting dead bodies. Between them, they'd manhandled Jay's enormous corpse out of the underground storeroom at the Major's impressive home by rolling him along on several wine barrels, taking it in turns to run to the back of the line of vats and scoot past the other to position another vat at the front whenever the make-shift conveyor belt was about to run out. They'd then persuaded a camel to its knees by feeding it a carrot that Adjo produced from a sleeve, before draping Jay across its back between the neck and the hump. With Adjo in the lead, they'd trotted the camel across the desert slopes to the dig site, whereupon the boy had snaffled the trestle table, a pair of lamps and a supply of formaldehyde from the foreman's office. Given that the foreman appeared to have been possessed by Seth, it didn't seem likely the items would be missed. And anyway, as Adjo had pointed out, what was a bit of theft after all the other crimes that had been recently been committed?

So now here they were, ready to begin the mummification of Albie's employer, friend and inspiration so that at least his spirit could live on in the afterlife. There seemed to be a sad lack of canopic jars anywhere, particularly the ones that Albie was accustomed to finding in Egyptian funerary practices which featured the heads of baboons to protect the lungs, or Qebehsenuef's falcon head to look over the intestines. In haste, Albie and Adjo had pelted around the dimly-lit cave, gathering wine ewers and any casket that didn't have a rat inside it and emptying the contents out under the trestle table.

Fortunately, Albie had remembered where his undertaker's tools were kept, so at least he was able to carry out the ceremony without using whatever knife Adjo could pilfer from the souk. The prospect of trying to draw Jay's brains out through his nose with a cocktail stirrer and a serving spoon would be too horrible to contemplate.

He sterilised his scalpel set in the candle flame. Jay might already be dead, but Albie still wanted to respect the body enough to ensure that nothing infected it ever again. Then he started as he had before, dragging the brain out of its chamber as if it were a jellyfish and chucking it into an emptied corn jar, and then moving on through the organs which he extracted carefully and settled into the makeshift canopic jars which Adjo sealed with candle wax.

Throughout the whole process, Albie muttered under his breath. 'I am the horned bull who rules the sky, Lord of Celestial Appearings, the Great Illuminator who came forth from the heat . . . I detest what is detestable. I will not eat faeces. I will not drink urine. I will not walk head downward . . .'

The jars were placed alongside the body on the table. 'I am loosed from my windings,' Albie went on, wishing they'd been able to find a coffin of some kind. Any kind. The closest they could manage was the trestle table with planks for the sides, which would have to be lashed on with cloth above Jay's bandaged body. 'I make ready the ferry boat of the sky; I eat of what they eat, I live on what they live, I have eaten bread in every pleasant room.'

'Master Cornthwaite,' hissed Adjo suddenly. 'What is that smell?'

Albie shook his head. 'Don't know. It could be Jay's poisoned flesh, or one of those dead rats, or even rotting food in the intestines. Take your pick.' He covered his nose with his sleeve; the stench really was vile.

But Adjo was peering over his shoulder. 'No, I don't think it's any of those things, although they do stink horrifically. I think it is some nasty green Seth breath.'

Of course. Around Albie's feet curled some disgusting tendrils of thick green gas, like a carpet of asps. 'Oh Lord. Already? I was much further along last time.'

He'd barely begun to position the scarab beetle over the heart. It was bad enough that they couldn't find any faience scarabs to do the job properly. Adjo had whittled one himself from a piece of wood and painted it blue, according to Albie's design. It was adding insult to injury that he wouldn't even be able to start the bandaging process before Seth's evil face appeared in the wall.

'Told you. It's going to be so much worse that last time, I know it,' he grumbled to Adjo, strapping the scarab to Jay's chest with crepe bandage from the first aid kit. They had only found one, so for the rest of the body they had torn up the sheet that had covered Jay in the cellar, which wouldn't make for a very neat job but was the best they could do in the circumstances, when nobody seemed to know anything about the materials used in mummification.

Albie sighed as he contemplated the scrappy pile of bindings. Was it even worth starting? He turned his head slightly as Adjo's eyes bulged. Sure enough, behind him a circle the colour of mucus was appearing on the limestone wall. At any second, Seth's porcine features would scratch themselves onto the surface and then grow and grow until it could swallow them whole, and then there'd be an explosion and all would be lost ...

Adjo raised a trembling finger towards the wall. 'He is here.'

'I know.' Staring down at Jay's half-mummified body, Albie felt tears sting his eyes behind his spectacles. 'I've failed you again, my friend,' he whispered. 'So sorry, dear chap.'

The putrid smell enveloped them. He could only see the whites of Adjo's eyes through the dank fog that resembled one of London's 'pea souper' smogs, and the remains of Jay were completely invisible. Over his shoulder, a swirling cylinder of evil loomed forth from the wall, spouting some nonsense that Albie couldn't even be bothered to listen to – all about his failure to raise Osiris and the curse that would follow them across the centuries, blah blah blah bulahhhh. He'd heard it all before, and as he seemed to be in some horrendous conundrum in time he might well hear it all again, and he couldn't stand it any longer.

'I know, I know!' he screamed, spinning around with the scalpel in his hand – not that it would damage Seth in any way, but it made him feel as if he was at least attempting to defend them all. 'I've failed and it's all over. You'll be ruler over everything and I'll be a mutant servant and it's all my own fault.'

The pig-head, vast and pustulous and vile, raised its snout and laughed, and then uttered the words that had been etched on Albie's brain for ever afterwards, to the extent that he could now repeat them at the same time as the tyrant before him:

'In underworld, in afterlife,
Eternal torment, endless strife,
Never more to be undone
Until two true hearts beat as one.'

'I know all that!' cried Albie, 'but what do you want me to do about it?'

He wasn't sure who he was asking. Adjo? Seth himself? Or perhaps Jay, whose investigations and meeting with Diselda had made the whole situation flare up in the first place.

'We tried, we really did,' he whispered to Jay, almost sobbing. 'Jack and I did everything we could – putting your heart together with Diselda's; finishing off Seth, or so we thought. Nothing has lifted the curse. Nothing has made things right. What else could I do, Jay?'

'Find the missing piece: Ozzy's crown,' cried a voice behind him.

That was strange. Why would Seth say that?

He spun around, sure that he'd recognised the voice. As he watched, Seth's evil, circular face split straight down the middle, and through the aperture, as if he were stepping through the pupil of an eye, stepped a golden-haired teenager.

Jack.

'Come on,' he said cheerfully. 'Let's get this mess sorted out. I think I know where Ozzy's crown is.' Jack peered around the cave. 'Great! Adjo, you're here too. You come along as well, and … is that Jay's mummy? Well, you might as well bring that along for the ride.'

'How did you get here?' spluttered Albie. 'And what happened to your hair?'

'Long story. Might take a while.' For some reason, this made Jack giggle. 'I'll explain it all once we've got Ozzy back together. Minty's here too, by the way. She's a bit ill so we'd better get a wiggle on.'

And before Albie could demand an explanation or even check that this fair-haired, tanned stranger was actually his friend, Jack Bootle-Cadogan, the pupil opened up further, spilling such blinding shafts of light into the cave that Adjo and Albie held their hands up to their eyes.

That was all it took. When they lowered them again, it was as if they'd never left Lowmount.

Chapter 18

Jack was almost as surprised as the others to find himself back at Lowmount. It was just as they'd left it. The roses still bloomed at the exact same rate and the setting sun was angled behind the castle much as he had seen it the day before they had Minty-travelled to their separate locations. Unless it was a whole year later, not much time had passed.

As if to prove that they were back in the twenty first century, Jack's phone buzzed in his pocket. Everyone started, as if they had all forgotten that such things existed, and it was only then that Jack realised he was staring at Bone, not Albie. He was holding his own phone in his skeletal fingers, glaring at it with such distaste that Jack half-expected his father's voice to rumble out of it.

Instead, they both checked their messages to find more or less the same text from Jack's mother. His actual mother. 'Your father's had one of his turns. Please head home.'

Jack sighed. 'I think Dad's been upsetting the National Trust volunteers again.'

Bone rolled his eyes. Obviously, he said without opening his mouth.

The group all stared at each other, trying to catch up with the events that had just brought them back together again. Minty leaned against Granny Dazzle's beloved tamarisk tree, her hair separating into lank strands. Beside her lay a reed basket, overflowing with chunks of green marble. Ajdo had aged a little, somehow – Jack guessed he was somewhere around his own age, or perhaps even a little more – and Albie had aged immeasurably, back to the bleary-purple-eyed butler he'd grown up with.

When Jack spotted what lay on the grass behind Bone, however, he sprang into action.

'Blimey!' he cried. 'I'd forgotten about Jay's half-mummified body. We'd better get him to the crypt and sort him out.'

Bone pointed to his mouth.

'Yes, and then you can talk again. And I'll explain what happened and we'll find Ozzy's crown. It's going to be a busy …' He checked his phone. 4.45pm, on the same day they'd left. Only a few hours had gone by although it had been days and weeks, centuries apart, for them – although after his meeting with the amazing Granny Nut, this was no longer a great surprise to him. 'A busy afternoon,' he finished.

Bone then pointed to Jack's head.

'Yes, I'll explain the hair.'

Ignoring Bone's smirk, which seemed to suggest that there could really be no reasonable explanation for hair like that other than having it bleached for boy-band stardom, Jack helped Minty to her feet and shouldered the rush basket. They followed Bone and Adjo with some astonishment as the two manoeuvred the solid box of Jay across Lowmount's gentle slopes towards the graveyard, rolling it along on logs from a tumble-down fence before using the Bentley like a fork-truck, with the front bumper bent into two right angles that slotted into the trestle's gaps. The pair were like a well-oiled machine themselves, communicating with a few nods and grunts as they laid out the whole plan wordlessly and efficiently. Just how long had they been in 1922? Not, thought Jack with another secretive smile, that time and location mattered. They'd obviously uncovered some partnership that transcended it all.

It was still a relief, however, to see Albie's bespectacled face peeking out from the crypt door as he and Minty staggered down the stone steps towards it. He's seen a lot on these steps: the jackals and ghosts that first indicated what he might be; Ozzy 'n' Ice and Ice 'n' Ozzy; even Bone smashing Guisely and Minty into a metal box made from the teacher's own car. Inside, of course, he'd met Granny Dazzle and his great grandfather, Jay, along with many other ancient relies. But nothing had really compared with discovering that Bone, his lifelong guide and companion, could be his friend and adviser, Albie, when they hung out in the crypt playing Senet, or mummifying the locals. It was totally not normal, but somehow it seemed like the most natural thing in the world to Jack.

He slapped Albie on the back as he entered the crypt. 'Nice work on Jay's coffin!'

'It's more of a stretcher, actually,' moaned Albie. 'I didn't expect to be bringing it back with me, of course, and I still can't understand why there were no funerary materials to hand.' He looked around the crypt with a deep sigh of relief. 'It's so good to be back among the mummified.'

'What do you mean?'

'I'll tell you while we finish the Opening of the Mouth Ceremony for Jay, and you can explain what happened to you. All of it,' said Albie with a nasty glance at Jack's head.

A voice interrupted them from behind the sarcophagus. 'Don't mind us. I'll just die here among some chunks of jade that I happen to know are the great god Osiris, and Adjo can get on with some sweeping or something.'

Jack laughed. 'Sorry, Minty. We should do this after we've found Ozzy's crown and sorted out Ma'at.'

'No rush,' she said sardonically, but it was evident from her reduced levels of sarcasm that there was some urgency around it.

So with Adjo's help, the familiar undertaking team of Jack and Albie quickly processed Jay through the parts of the ceremony he'd missed. To their relief, they were barely through the final words when Jay's ba rose majestically from his body and reached out a hand. Instantly the ba of Diselda Carruthers, as beautiful as she had been in 1922, filtered through the stone top of the sarcophagus and joined

Jay in an embrace. Together again, they beamed at everyone around them and then made way for the next vital ceremony to begin.

It was the most critical one of all, and Jack gave it his full respect.

'This piece,' he said, laying Ozzy's foot on the lid of the family grave, 'brought the miracle of wheat to a starving village.'

He put the pieces of jade together like an immense 3d jigsaw, describing every miracle that Ozzy had managed to create even when it seemed that Seth had thwarted him.

'This was the last part,' Jack said, placing the hand that had pointed to a spring into position. 'And I still hadn't found Ozzy's crown. Or so I thought until I saw Minty leaning against a tree.'

Minty was huddled beneath a candle, gently stroking Hathor's chest feathers. The flickering light cast dark shadows beneath her eyes, and Jack realised just how ill she had become.

'Don't look at me,' she barked to Albie and Adjo who had both turned to her expectantly. 'He keeps saying this, but I haven't got it.'

'No, but you had it. You just didn't know it.'

Minty glared at him. 'What? You're talking in riddles, like Nephthys.'

'That's right,' cried Jack excitedly. 'Nephthys started it all off, to help her sister!'

As if he'd summoned her, Nephthys and Ice appeared on either side of the crypt's small altar, both looking regal and grown-up. Albie gasped at the sight of Ice with her cow-horn headdress, and he and Adjo both lowered their heads in a bow. Nephthys caught Jack's eye, and nodded slightly in his direction.

He had worked it out.

It was the moment to bring Ozzy back to his full self.

'If you can,' he said quickly, 'come with me. If you can't, don't worry; we'll be back in a few minutes.'

To his amazement, they all insisted on coming with him, even Jay and Granny Dazzle who risked being blown away in the wind, and Minty who was getting more grey and slick with perspiration by the second. Grabbing any humans that he could, Jack transformed into Anubis, not caring that it was barely dusk and he might be seen by a passing villager, or even someone from school. Some things were just more important than looking normal. Then he focussed on where they needed to be, a firm hand on Bone and Adjo's shoulders, and Zipped back across the graveyard and the rolling landscape at the edges of the castle's grounds, in exactly the route they'd taken to reach the crypt a short while ago.

The sky was oppressive overhead, with the promise of an early autumn storm. Jack smiled as the wind whipped around his ears, and quickly changed himself back into a young man.

'It's been here all along,' he said, and the others followed his gaze to where Ozzy's crown had lain for decades and decades, maybe even a century. They just wouldn't have been able to locate it until Jack had understood the concept of the now, which couldn't have happened until he met Grandmother Nut, which couldn't have happened unless he'd gone to protect Ozzy, which couldn't have happened if Ozzy and Ice hadn't appeared to him on the crypt steps … Time and space meant nothing. All that he needed was what he knew in his heart, which he could feel with the intensity of the light the Sky Goddess had drawn around him.

He turned to the tamarisk tree. 'Who planted this tree?'

A wavering wisp of pale blue chiffon raised a hand.

'Yes, Granny Dazzle, it was you. These were the seeds in a locket that you gave to someone special – your heart on a string.' Jay's arm flew up triumphantly, and Jack laughed. 'Yes, to you, Jay. But who,' he continued, 'gave you the locket, Granny Dazzle?'

'That … that was me,' said Minty. 'As instructed by …' She turned to point. 'Nephthys!'

As they all stared at her, Nephthys had the grace to blush. 'It is complex, I know, but it could not be directly done. I was doing the bidding of my own mother, the Sky Goddess, Nut, to protect us all.'

Jack nodded carefully. 'Yes, and I've now met the Sky Goddess, Nut, and I understand it a bit. It matters that we're all together. It matters that we're all involved. It matters only that it's now, not where and when it happened. Um, I think we should hold hands.'

'You want me to hold hands?' said Bone without saying a word, but then Jack saw that his rheumy eyes were bulbous with envy. You met the Sky Goddess! That was what he would have said if he could mime it.

With a smile, Jack turned to the tamarisk tree. One by one, they surrounded the tree and linked hands, ghostly fingers with human ones, godly arms joining spirit and boy together in a chain that stretched around it and up towards its branches.

'Now,' he said firmly, 'could I please have the crown of Osiris?'

It was just as it had been in the Byblos palace grounds. Even just as it had been when Nephthys had first appeared beside him. The leaves of Granny Dazzle's most adored tree shimmied and shivered in the heightening wind as the very knots of bark intertwined in an exotic dance. Boles and knots moved and exchanged places, moved and exchanged places, until suddenly a hole appeared in the broadest part of the trunk of tree. From its depths, a slender wooden tendril extended, and on it, as if the tree were balancing it on a finger, dangled a conical headdress in vibrant white, topped with the same golden disk as Ice's crown and flanked by the twin plumes of a pair of ostrich feathers.

Bone's mouth opened and shut like one of the castle's sash windows. He nudged Adjo in the ribs, and he hissed obligingly: 'The Atef Crown!' Then he laughed. 'That really is a treasure, like the name of Adjo!'

As gently as possible in case the tree decided to swallow the crown and half his arm as he'd seen with Ozzy's coffin, Jack eased the pointed headdress from the twig on which it balanced and clutched it to his chest. Instantly the tree seemed to release a deep, shuddering sigh – although surely it was the wind in the leaves above? – and the bark rearranged itself again as the slender branch withdrew once more into the trunk of the tamarisk tree.

'We've got it,' said Jack, hardly able to believe it himself although he was holding the thing in his hands. It thrummed like his meteorite dagger, a strange and potent mixture of earthly ostrich feathers and solidified starlight …

'Let's finish this,' he said.

Across space, across Lowmount, Ice and Nephthys transported them. Mere moments later, they stood before the broken statue of Osiris. Jack reached over to place the crown back on the fragmented statue, but suddenly thought better of it.

'Ice, this is your job,' he said quietly. And then, with a respectful nod, he continued: 'Your job it is.'

Overwhelmed, Ice's brilliant blue eyes turned liquid. For a moment Jack thought it might be too much for her and he stepped forward again to take the Atef Crown from her trembling fingers, but she shook her head.

'My tears are in gratitude to you, not fear. We thank you, Jack.'

Well. That made him feel a little tearful himself, if the truth were told. Jack distracted them all by adjusting Ozzy's head, ready to receive the crown, even though it had been perfectly straight before, and it wasn't as if Ozzy had leapt up and danced a jig while they'd been out urging the tamarisk tree to cough up its contents.

'That's better,' he said, as Albie smothered a snigger. 'Now, Ice.'

The sarcophagus was tall. Jack remembered a time when Ice had barely reached its centre, but now it was no obstacle for the goddess. Raising the crown until it was on a level with her own ornate headdress, Ice drifted up from the floor of the crypt until she hovered beside Ozzy's head.

'In Ra, in Aten, in Nut and Geb, I restore you, Great Osiris,' she said calmly.

Then she placed the crown in position where the jagged hole of Ozzy's scalp had always been visible.

Phosphorescent light suddenly filled the room, emanating from the white apex of Ozzy's crown in an array of laser beams that crossed and flittered into a beautiful latticework. Lacy with light, the lattice hovered beneath the ceiling and then drifted down in a gauzy net which enveloped the marble pieces of Osiris. The others watched, awe-struck, as the light lattice draped itself over the prone statue, then tucked itself in around the body and gently turned it over and over as it lifted it from the sarcophagus, wrapping Ozzy into a cocoon so bright that they could barely look at it. Only when there was no jade marble to be seen through the silver-white gossamer did the body begin to float back onto its plinth ... but this time the statue pivoted in mid-air so that it came to rest on its feet. Even through the covering, it was possible to see the outline of Osiris, proud and upright with this crook in one hand and his flail in the other, positioned across his chest with the tops just touching the ostrich feathers on either side of the Atef Crown.

'It is him!' cried Ice. 'Him it is!'

Jack looked on as Ice and Nephthys ran forward, clawing at the cocoon with their fingers. It melted away beneath their touch; suddenly there was the Pharaoh he had met in the palace, regal and imposing and only faintly green. Ice clapped her hands with joy. 'He is restored!'

'We've done it, old chap,' said a voice behind Jack.

He turned to find Albie dabbing a handkerchief beneath his spectacles. Ha. So he wasn't the only one who found it all moving. 'We've only gone and done it.'

'Looks like it,' said Jack, but then he noticed that Albie wasn't looking at him. Instead his friends' eyes were focussed on the applauding ghosts of Jay and Diselda.

For a long moment, Jay and Albie stared at each other, and then, nodding graciously, Jay turned his hands towards Albie and clapped directly to him. Diselda joined in, and

Albie gave up on trying to hold back the tears. They cascaded down his cheeks as Adjo slapped first him and then Jack on the back, belching out great shouts of laughter and a torrent of Egyptian epithets that Jack had no chance of following.

The two goddesses were hugging joyfully, but of the third goddess, there was no sign. Then suddenly Minty strode past him in glorious full health, her hair a shiny helmet once more and her hawk perched on the skullcap she wore in a way that had obviously become too painful for her of late.

'That feels so much better,' said Minty as she flung open the crypt door. 'And look!'

Hathor gave a little shudder and then stretched his wings, flapping upwards and outwards over the graveyard and into the canopy of the trees beyond. Even from this distance, it was evident that the trees had just enjoyed a massive growth spurt, and the weeds around the gravestones were so rampant that many of the tombs had disappeared beneath the foliage. Disturbed by the sudden growth, the ghostly occupants of the graves were filtering up from the graves to see what was going on. Percy the Gardener was scratching his head in such agitation that it might have suggested an imminent heart attack, if he wasn't already dead.

'It's like this all over Lowmount!' reported Minty, using Hathor's vision as he swooped across the estate. 'The lake is overflowing and ... oh, Jack. Your mother's tropical plants have burst through the roof of the greenhouse. Thought I'd better warn you.'

'Amazing,' said Jack, staring at the ghosts among the greenery as they high-fived or joined up for a little dance here and there.

Everybody, especially the non-bodies, was celebrating. Which was quite as it should be, of course, thought Jack, as they'd spent all this time – in some cases, a lifetime or more – trying to make this happen. Ozzy's crown had been found, and he was restored. The verdant explosion of the Lowmount grounds and the glossy ebony of Minty's hair was testament to that.

So why didn't he feel like whooping for joy and joining in the celebrations himself?

There was something wrong.

Jack stared up at Ozzy. 'Are you coming down from there?'

The Pharaoh continued to stare straight ahead of him, peaceful and noble.

'Ozzy? Why aren't you moving?'

There was no reply from above him, and suddenly the crypt fell quiet as the others worked out what Jack had just said.

Ozzy wasn't moving. He was whole and glowing and vibrantly green, but it was as though he was still a statue. As if hearing Jack's thoughts, the threads of gossamer light wound themselves around Ozzy's form again and laid him gently on the sarcophagus. He looked like an effigy on top of a tomb.

Perhaps, Jack realised with a sinking heart, he actually was an effigy on top of a tomb.

'What's … what's going on?' he whispered. 'Why hasn't it worked?'

Albie pushed his spectacles back up his nose and inspected the Ozzy statue. 'Oh damnation and tribulations and an infinite number of blast-its,' he said mournfully. 'It. Isn't. Over.' His head sank onto the sarcophagus.

'But it must be! We found the crown. He's all glowy and green. And Minty looks amazing again!' Ouch. Why had he said that? Anyway. Jack ploughed on, feeling unexpectedly furious. 'It has to have worked. It has to! I can't still be cursed! I refuse! Ice, what's happ—'

He was interrupted by two things: firstly, the familiar keening of Ice in distress – a low moan like an animal in pain that told him all was not right. Ozzy was not restored, or at least not in any way that they truly recognised. He wasn't, for instance, alive.

The second interruption, however, was even more concerning. Through the open door walked a familiar and frightening figure.

'Jack!' barked his father. 'What in the name of all that's holy are you doing down here? You'll start a ruddy fire with all these candles, and I can't see the insurance covering that! Or are you smoking something? That might explain your erratic behaviour recently. Good gravy, boy, what's happened to your hair?'

Jack gulped. 'Dad? What ... I come here a lot,' he said, as if that explained the new effigy on the tomb and a group of people partying around it. Not that his father would be able to see most of them ...

But perhaps he was wrong. Squinting up at the ceiling, Lord Bootle-Cadogan's mouth fell open. 'What the blazes ... Gramps, is that you? And G ... Granny?' He spun around to Minty and Adjo, spluttering, 'Who are you? You! Girl! You look familiar!'

And then at last he noticed Albie, who had lifted his head blearily from the tomb and was staring at Jack's father, aghast.

'Saints preserve us,' gasped Jackson Bootle-Cadogan. 'You're ... I've seen photographs. I know who you are. You're bloody Bone!' His gaze raced up and down Albie as if he expected him to burst into his tailcoat and bald head persona at any second. 'This is bally outrageous.'

'Dad, what are you doing here?' said Jack at long last.

'I came to get you,' roared his father, rounding on him. 'You didn't respond to your mother's text and now I see why. Far too busy having parties in the family crypt! Outrageous! Well, you need to stop your bally messing about and get up to the bally castle immediately. Imm-ed-iate-ly, d'ye hear me? Your mother needs you. Now!'

With a last penetrating glare at Albie, Lord Bootle-Cadogan swivelled on his heel and marched out of the crypt, disappearing into the gathering gloom in the graveyard. 'You!' they heard him screech. 'Out of my blessed way!'

'Who does he think he's talking to!' cried Albie. '*He's outrageous.*'

Jack shook his head. 'But that's just it. Who is he talking to?' He ran to the door beside Minty and peered out into the darkness. Percy and Vera were attempting to untangle some Japanese Knotweed from Vera's tombstone, and various of the other graveyard residents were taking the opportunity to chat and catch up with each other. Of a real live person, there was no sign. 'There's nobody out there. No actual body at all.'

With a growing sense of doom in his gut, Jack flung open the door behind the altar that led to the secret passage he'd used so many times before. Between his two homes. Between his two lives. Followed by a trail of people and non-people, Jack ran for one of those lives, faster than he'd ever gone before.

Chapter 19

He found his mother in her study, clutching Roger around the neck so hard that the dog's eyes were protruding. She was staring at the wall, saying over and over, 'I don't know what to do. I don't know what to do. Where is Bone? And Jack? I don't know what to do.'

'Mum, I'm here,' he cried, checking in the polished door that he looked like her teenage son and not her much-loved hound before skidding into the room. 'What's the matter?'

He was about to explain that he'd just seen his father and had been sent to find her, but something told him that this would be a mistake. His parents rarely saw eye to eye, especially where Jack was concerned, so it would be better to suggest that he'd only just seen her message.

But when she turned to him, her face a pale mask of grief, she shoved Roger off her lap and hurried over to him, pushing his head against her shoulder.

'Oh, Jack! You're too late! You weren't in time. You should have come when I texted.'

'What's happened?'

She buried her face in her hands. 'Your father. He's ... he died, Jack!'

Jack stared at her, his insides caving. But he can't have done, he wanted to say. I just saw him. He just told me off, like he always does, and he sent me here, and ...

'But he ... he was fine,' he whispered.

'He wasn't!' squeaked his mother, barely able to hold back her tears. 'He ate too much and drank too much and I kept warning him, I did, Jack, every time he had one of his bilious attacks. But then this morning he said he didn't feel too well so he went back to bed, and this afternoon I went to deliver his soup to him and he was just lying there in his room. White. Stony white. Like a statue!'

'But what happened?'

'A heart attack, Jack. The doctor tells me he won't have felt much – just a sharp pain in his chest. He looks – surprised, and not a little angry.' His mother almost laughed, but it turned to sobs instead. 'How like Jackson to be cross about it! I bet he'll have something to say to Saint Peter or whoever greets him at the Pearly Gates.'

Jack nodded mutely, a tear trickling down his cheek as he put his arms around his mother. How strange that she was suddenly so much smaller than him, even in his normal teenager form. She felt frail and thin as she leaned against him, and Jack's heart felt as though it might give out, too, with all the pain that stabbed through it. He had to comfort her, somehow, and suddenly he knew how.

He thought of his father glaring at Albie. Of course he had stared: he hadn't seen Albie as a person before, only as Bone the manservant. And it was only because he was ... Jack couldn't bring himself to say it yet ... because of his *condition* that he'd been able to see Albie at all – and Jay, Diselda, Percy and Vera.

'He'll have a go at anyone who gets in his way,' he said. 'Anyone he thinks has ever wronged him, he'll be giving them a roasting.'

'I know!' His mother was half-laughing, half-crying. 'Whether he was right or not!'

'He'll be very glad to see some people again, though, like his grandpa Jay and Granny Dazzle.'

She sniffed. 'He always was ridiculously fond of her. And he absolutely revered Jay and their long, long happy marriage.'

'And as for anyone else, they'd just better stay out of his way,' said Jack gently. 'Lord Bootle-Cadogan, coming through!' he cried in a bad impersonation of his father shouting at Percy the Gardener.

The second he mentioned his father's title, however, Jack's innards clenched. Lord Bootle-Cadogan. Oh no, no, no. Not now. Not this. He so wasn't ready. He hadn't planned to be ready ever, but certainly not now. No!

'Mum,' he said urgently, 'does that mean I'm now, you know …'

At this point, she gave in completely to the flood of tears that had been threatening to engulf her since he'd arrived. 'Ye-e-e-es,' she wailed. 'Lord of Lowmount – my little boy! How can that be? Surely that's not meant to be! You're just a child. Oh, Jack; I don't know what to do!'

But with a sudden flash of insight, Jack knew exactly what to do. He might still be young, but he definitely wasn't just a child. He was a lot more besides, and he couldn't help feeling that all the skills and lessons he'd learned in his role as Anubis had all been leading to this point. He didn't have to be Lord Bootle-Cadogan ... as long as the previous one was still alive.

He could talk to his father! Persuade him back into his body, somehow. Albie could help. Heck, Ice and Nephthys could chip in too. In fact, by the time he got back to the crypt he was pretty sure that Ozzy would be striding around being green and luminous, and he had to be useful in bringing someone back to life who, let's face it, had only very recently had a heart attack.

'Where's Dad now?' he asked his mother, hoping he hadn't been taken to the hospital. He knew where part of him was – his ba was striding around Lowmount, snapping orders at unwary ghosts – but he'd have to find the physical part of him to try to coax his spirit back into his body.

'He's ... Did you want to see him? Oh, Jack, I'm so sorry. I didn't think you'd want to see him like ... like that. But the doctor had already been and he called Bone at the undertakers'. I was waiting for him so that we could just get on with it. Jackson would have wanted me to just get on with it.'

Jack hugged her again, the pain of her anguish almost worse than that of finding out his father had died. He wished he could tell her it was going to be okay. He himself was just going to get on with it.

'I'm going to take care of it all, Mum,' he told her carefully. There, that didn't give too much away. 'Maybe the doctor was wrong,' he added, just to prepare her for seeing her husband alive and shouty again.

She stared at him. 'Of course he wasn't wrong. I saw him myself, Jack. He ... I can't explain it, really; Jackson just wasn't in his body any more. Oh!' she howled. 'You're in denial. It's one of the five stages of grief. I should have let you see him!'

For the slightest of moments, Jack wished he could ring a bell and have Bone appear with a cup of tea. Bone always knew how to make things right. But now Bone had a new role, and as the undertaker he had already been summoned. Good. That was going to make things easier.

'I'll get you some tea,' he said, lowering her gently into the chair again and placing Roger's slobbering face on her lap. She took one look at the dog and broke into a fresh round of sobs.

'You were always his dog, really, Roger. Jackson's. Thank goodness we're not like those Egyptians who buried their pets with the owners when they died. I couldn't bear to lose you both. Oh!'

Jack held his breath. If she had even the slightest inkling that they were, in fact, exactly like those very Egyptians, he might have more than one parent to revive. Once he was sure she wasn't looking, he changed himself into Doghead, Zipped to the kitchen for tea with lots of sugar in it (as Bone would have made at times of shock) and transported it back to the study, transforming as he entered with the tea tray.

'Thank you, darling,' his mother said shakily, gazing up at him with a tear-streaked face. 'Oh my word. I hadn't noticed – what have you done to your hair?'

His hair? Had he forgotten to change his head? He glanced in the silver tray and saw his hair, ground to a bright yellow by the sands of Ancient Egypt. 'Oh. I dyed it,' he said quickly. 'Thought I might audition for the school's boy band.'

Before she could tell him how much his father would have scoffed at that, he dropped a kiss onto the top of her head and backed out of the room just as the enormous doorbell clanged. To his relief, his mother did not appear to answer it, but one of the National Trust ladies came out of the formal dining room, clutching a soggy tissue.

'Oh, Jack ... I mean, Lord ...'

'Claire, it's fine. I mean, there's no need for all that. I'm going to get the door and take care of all the undertaking things. Would you check in on my mother?'

She nodded tearfully; Jack gave her a tiny shove to get rid of her more quickly and then skidded to the door on the polished oak floorboards.

On the doorstep stood Bone, cap in hand and a strange expression on his pallid face. Behind him, his undertaker's hearse idled on the gravel forecourt.

'Good!' cried Jack enthusiastically.

Grabbing Bone by the lapels before he could protest, he Zipped them both to his father's bedroom so quickly that they stumbled into the room, barely avoiding toppling onto the bed.

Jack stopped abruptly, his ribs suddenly hurting. He'd been so carried away with the thought of resurrecting his father that he'd almost forgotten that he'd already died. How could this ... this body in his father's pyjamas actually be his dad? Without all his bluster and vigour, he looked calmer but somehow diminished in size. His hand still lay across his chest where he'd clutched at his heart. Bone took one look at it before crossing to the bedside with his back carefully positioned between Jack and his father. When he straightened again, the offending arm was tucked under the bedclothes, and Jackson's eyes were closed.

'Thanks, Al-Bone,' said Jack. 'But I'm okay. Because you and I are going to take my father to the crypt and collect his ba on the way, and then we're going to put him back together.'

No. Bone shook his head, then mimed driving his own hearse to his own undertaker's quarters.

'It'll be fine. I'm sure Ozzy is back to full strength now – I think Dad's ...' He couldn't bring himself to say ghost. '... Dad appearing like that probably interrupted the process.'

No, no. Bone's head-shaking was both insistent and annoying.

'Yes. And with several goddesses and a few undertakers and – well, me, we'll be able to pop Dad's ba back inside him and just send him back to his old self.'

Bone's head practically shook itself off his neck. No, no, no, no, and an infinite number of nos.

Jack laughed in disbelief. 'You can't be serious? You hold so much of a grudge against my father that you won't help to bring him back to life?'

At that, Bone looked hurt. He glared at Jack with his strange violet eyes, then strode over to the bed again and hoisted Jackson, complete with bedding, over his shoulder. He jerked his head at the door, and Jack worked out what he meant.

'Sorry,' he muttered. 'Didn't mean that. It's just ... he's my dad, you know.'

He felt dangerously like crying, so he stopped himself by gripping Bone's gloved hand and Zipping them down the corridor towards the castle museum. Halfway there, he stopped and turned them around, back towards the front door and the driveway. 'Better go in your car, he said. 'Otherwise Mum will wonder what's happened. I don't want anything else to bother her.'

He would put it right for her soon. She'd be amazed and overjoyed when her husband walked back through the door, ready to be his irascible old self for another twenty years or so. Ready for Jack to be old enough to even think about taking over as Lord of Lowmount.

They drove silently around the estate, taking the back lanes so that the hearse wouldn't be spotted by any of the castle's staff, and entering the graveyard from the roadside. To his relief, Bone had a proper undertaker's gurney and even a coffin to put his father into, so they didn't have to drag him along on a makeshift trolley, open to the skies.

As they entered the crypt, Jack held his breath, hoping with everything he could muster that Osiris would meet them with a nod of his weirdly-bearded head. His optimism was short-lived, however. Inside, Ozzy's effigy still lay on top of the BC family sarcophagus. Bone even had to shift him over a little to make room for Jack's father – although inside the crypt, he was Albie once more, pinched in the face and so cross with Jack that he could barely look at him.

From their position near the candle sconces, Minty and Adjo raised their heads from where they had clearly been offering prayers to Ra.

'Sorry about your father, Jack,' said Minty.

'How did you know?'

Minty pointed to the hawk resting on the crown of her head. 'I guessed when he came in here earlier, and then Hathor confirmed it.'

'Well, I've come to fix it.' Jack looked around for his father's Ba. 'Have you seen his spirit anywhere? Hathor, can you see it?'

In a strange, synchronised movement, Minty and Hathor shook their heads, and finally Albie spoke up.

'You do know that it's not a good idea to try to mess with nature to this degree, don't you?' he blurted. 'Mummification is one thing. Resurrection is quite another.'

'It's my dad,' said Jack simply. 'I have all of you, and all these skills. I have to try.'

'Really? And what would you like your beloved father to be? A zombie? The undead? Or perhaps immortal, so that you never have to take his place as Lord.' Albie folded his arms crossly.

'It's not that …' wailed Jack, although he had to admit that a tiny part of him had considered that. 'Why are you so mad with me?'

Albie rolled his eyes. 'Because it's the same all over again! My family all died and that was that. Gone.'

'We sent them through the Field of Rushes,' Jack pointed out.

'Yes, but just their spirits. We didn't start messing around with their bodies.'

'Yes we did,' said Jack, hardly believing what he was hearing. What a time to attack him! 'We laid your own brother out on that slab there, and had to fight him off in the graveyard.'

'That was Seth, not us!' screamed his friend.

'Albie,' said Jack quickly, 'what are you on about? Why are you so cross?'

To his horror, his friend's eyes filled with tears. 'Because I lost them all, Jack. Everyone but you. I couldn't save my brother Will, or my own mother. I couldn't even prevent Diselda from missing her husband so much because I was just this mute ... idiot who didn't know how to propose to her properly. And most of all, I couldn't save Jay. Even in the second time of trying, I couldn't save Jay! I had no life, Jack. No life apart from being a servant to your family. And I thought the curse would be over by now and I would be truly free, but it's not. I'm still doing your family's bidding!'

'All right!' screamed Jack. 'I free you! I'm the head of this family now and I free you from ever having to deal with us again if it disgusts you so much!'

'Okay, here I go! Look, I'm free, so I'm just going to walk out of that door and go and be ... a botanist! Or a greengrocer. Watch!'

With an appalling grin like someone who'd lost his mind, Albie marched through the doorway – but it was as if the silky net of Osiris lay across it, because Albie was instantly bounced back into the crypt.

'Ah, so not a greengrocer. I'm just going to get married to a ... a doctor, and be a kept man!' he announced, and barged again towards the graveyard. Once more he was pushed back by whatever force was barring the doorway. He forced his way through it, transformed instantly into Bone, and stomped back into the crypt to change back into Albie.

Finally, Albie shook his head sadly. 'I'm sorry. It's not your fault. But don't you see – it's not your doing at all. You're still under the curse yourself. We're not free, either of us. We're still under the spell of Seth.'

Jack stopped short, thinking hard. Of course. What Albie said was true. He'd thought restoring Osiris was the key, but if it had been, he wouldn't be able to transform into Doghead. He'd just be an ordinary – sort of – teenager.

'I don't know what to do,' he whispered, echoing his mother. 'Tell me, someone.'

As if they were answering his prayers, Ice and Nephthys materialised at the altar. Ice was calm again, breathing normally and able to look at Ozzy's effigy without breaking down. They both glanced at Lord Bootle-Cadogan's body beside it with a complete lack of curiosity, and then nodded to Jack.

'It is Ma'at,' said Nephthys.

'What is?'

Ice sighed with the chill of a January storm. 'This is the natural order of things. The Great Osiris must make way for a new and worthy king.'

'Someone young, strong and true,' agreed Nephthys.

'Oh no, you don't,' said Jack. 'It's bad enough I have to grow hairy dog ears and be an English lord. I'm not going to rule over Ancient Egypt as well. No way.'

The goddesses laughed together. 'Who can say? The chosen one, Horus, will banish Seth forever and be a great Pharaoh in Osiris' place,' said Nephthys.

That didn't sound like a no to him. 'I'm not being Pharaoh,' he said in a huff.

'We shall see what we shall see,' said Ice in her strange calm manner. 'But this much we do know. For now, Jackanubis, this is your task: for Osiris's spirit to pass through the Field of Rushes so that he can become the ruler of Duat, he must be carefully processed as you know how to do. You—' She turned to Albie. '—and your dearest friend, between you.'

Jack took a moment to work out what they were saying. When he did, he felt a little unsteady on his feet. It was almost worse than having to be Pharaoh and the grandson of a Sky Nut. 'We have to mummify Ozzy?'

The sisters nodded, as Albie let out a gasp.

'Of course!' he cried, slapping the sarcophagus. 'That's why there were no coffins or canopic jars or any of the stuff to mummify Jay. Mummification hadn't been invented!'

'What do you mean? Who invented mummification?' asked Jack, perplexed.

Albie laughed. 'You did, Jackanubis. Don't you see? Osiris was the first mummy. When you went back to his dynasty and interrupted the flow of time, Ozzy wasn't mummified and the process didn't start to happen. There were no mummies, or shabti, or sarcophagi, or canopic jars or anything.'

'No resting place for Osiris!' crowed Adjo. 'That is why we could not find him.'

'You have to do it, Jack,' said Albie. 'Tonight. We have to do it. Or ---'

'—it will never end!' finished Adjo.

It was horrific. Utterly horrific. Of course he was used to the mummification process and the various ceremonies he had to perform as Anubis, but to do it to Ozzy – to his friend – was simply horrendous.

But the Jack saw the expressions of everyone around him. Albie, poor Albie, had already tried to mummify his friend. Twice. Minty had nearly died without Osiris's positive powers, and what would happen if someone didn't pick up the reins? As for Ice and Nephthys – well, they had travelled the length and breadth of the African continent searching for Ozzy. They'd ventured through time to come to Lowmount, to seek the crown of Osiris.

And suddenly he saw how interlinked it all was. How he had played a part in it all, from the beginnings of their search to this moment. He couldn't let them down now.

He ran a hand across his face. 'Okay,' he said. 'Tonight. I'll go and see my mother and make sure she's okay, and then I'll meet you all back here and we'll ... mummify Osiris, and see what I can do about my dad. But after that, I'm serious.' He pointed at the ceiling, hoping he was reaching his weird grandmother – either of them. 'After that, I just want to be normal. Do you hear me?'

A shaft of light beamed across the crypt. Someone was listening, he was sure of it.

The only problem was that he wasn't quite sure who.

Chapter 20

They worked long into the night, taking the gentlest and most reverential care of the Pharaoh's body as they prepared it for the Afterlife. Muttering their incantations, Jack and Albie removed the brain, the lungs, the liver and spleen that all still glowed with a faint green hue. Adjo, who had volunteered to help them and who seemed to be able to stomach anything that was shoved at him with an easy acceptance, ran around with sterilised canopic jars and precious anointing oils, while Minty guarded the door in case any marauding ghosts – or pigs – decided to drop in.

Finally, Jack placed an amulet shaped like a scarab beetle over Ozzy's heart.

'I make ready the ferry boat of the sky; I eat of what they eat, I live on what they live, I have eaten bread in every pleasant room,' murmured Albie.

Jack loomed over Osiris, taller than ever in his Anubis form. He was having yet another growth surge - he only hoped it wasn't because he was about to become ruler of Egypt.

'Farewell, my friend,' he said into Ozzy's ear. 'I'll see your ba on the other side. And I'm sure you'll do an excellent job of ruling Duat.'

For a second, he and Albie gazed at each other, communicating in the Bone-speak that had connected them since Jack was born. Ready? Albie's face appeared to say. Jack raised an eyebrow. As I'll ever be. As I could ever be to be consigning a friend to eternity, even if it is in the Field of Rushes and beyond.

They nodded at the same moment and then began the long, intricate process of embalming the body in salts and oils before wrapping it in bandages in a steadily pleasing formation. It would have been easier if Ozzy could have done it himself like the lattice of light, but it was evident to all of them that the Pharaoh was no longer truly connected with his body. It was like seeing his father lying in the bed – as if he was there on the outside but the insides had left.

With the bandaging completed, Jack finally allowed Ice and Nephthys into the room. Before them they pushed the simple wooden casket that would hold Osiris, hopefully for eternity, with the letters 'ADJO' carved into the lid.

'That means "Treasure"!' cried Adjo happily. 'And also, me!'

'Well, it didn't work before, but hopefully this will keep Osiris safe from harm.' Albie stopped to tuck the last end of bandage into a fold, and then moved closer to scoop up the body with Jack on the other side.

Ice, however, waved them aside. 'Let me,' she said.

Jack had never seen her so steady, although her pale blue eyes had darkened into sapphire pools that reminded him of the sink-hole at their last temple – bottomless and dark.

With a wave of her arm she raised Osiris' body into the air. It drifted slowly across the crypt towards the ceiling, so that Adjo and Jack could slide the coffin into place on top of the family tomb. She drew back her arm and the mummy began to descend, gently and effortlessly, into the wooden casket. Once it was safely ensconced in there, Ice removed a broad golden bracelet from her upper arm and placed it beside him. 'You can return it when we meet again.'

She stepped back, allowing the three young men to stow all around and across Ozzy's mummy the items that would assist him in the afterlife: the organs that would be used again; the beautifully detailed image of his face that Nephthys had produced, so that his ba would recognise his physical vessel; the shabti, models of the devoted staff who would delight in serving him in Duat.

Finally, when it seemed there was nothing left to do but seal up the casket, Albie popped in one final shabti. 'I made that one in my own likeness,' he said, 'so that if I do ever dig you up again, you'll recognise me.'

'Aw,' moaned Jack. 'I haven't got him anything.'

'You look like a half a dog,' retorted Albie. 'He'll always recognise you. And you definitely get to see him again.'

'True.'

There was nothing more to be done – on this side of the earthly plane, at any rate. With the strength of Anubis,

Jack pushed aside the sarcophagus lid and lowered the coffin into it.

'Over to you,' he said to Ice and Nephthys.

As the two sisters reached across the sarcophagus with arms extended and linked hands, a familiar green mist began to rise from the tomb, the shades shifting from the deepest sage of a forest leaf through the brightest emerald to the faintest tint of a fish scale before the whole tomb lit up from within. The goddesses' eyes glowed with the same green, lasering across the crypt to alight on each of their faces in turn, and then the brightness intensified until even Jack could no longer look at it.

When they opened their eyes, the mummy and the two goddess guardians had disappeared.

The crypt seemed disarmingly empty, as if more than just the coffin had gone from it.

'Shall I open the door?' said Minty. 'I feel like I need to let some warmth in.'

'Just no evil gods, okay?'

'Obviously.'

She pulled on the handle and they all stared out into the darkness, trying to see if anything had changed. It all looked pretty normal, but somehow Jack knew that something had fundamentally shifted. Nothing was ever going to be quite the same again.

'Don't you have something to do?' said Albie suddenly. 'I'd love to do it for you, only I'm not a god.'

Adjo beamed. 'Ah, Mr Albie, don't put yourself down. You have done many great things, Just now, you have saved a kingdom.'

'Why, yes I have.' Albie winked at Jack. 'That's going to be my new job title. Kingdom saver.'

Jack stretched to his full height. 'In that case, I'd better check we did actually save the king.'

It was pre-arranged. Once Ozzy's mummy had disappeared, Jackanubis (which seemed to be catching on among his friends) was to travel to the underworld for the Weighing of the Heart against the Feather of Thoth, and then, assuming that was okay, he'd meet Ozzy at the Field of Rushes.

Once upon a time, he'd dreaded the journey to the underworld, and had almost died trying to achieve it. Now – he laughed as he thought of the word – Jack knew enough about a certain Sky Goddess and the limitlessness of her abilities that he realised he only had to ask for her help, and she would transport him.

Just before he left, however, he held out his arms. 'Group hug,' he said with a grin. 'Come on. We've been through a lot today, and I think we should bring it in.'

'First holding hands and now group hugs. We drew the line at double-handed handshakes in my day, Jack,' grumbled Albie, but he stood up anyway, propping one arm across Adjo's shoulders and the other around Jack's back. Albie grabbed Minty's hand and slotted her in between them; a little sheepishly, Jack put his arm around her. To his astonishment, she didn't flinch. He wondered if she would flinch or even punch him if he sniffed her hair.

Seriously, what was wrong with him?

'Thank you,' he said gruffly, hoping nobody had noticed his quivering black nose. 'I feel like we should have a team motto or something.'

'Don't kick the dog?' suggested Albie.

Everybody laughed, even Jack, who considered it a miracle considering the day he'd just had.

'I'd better get going,' he said, almost reluctantly.

But before he could lower his arms, a rush of pungent, acrid air, like rotting corpses and raw sewage, swept into the crypt with such force that they all slid over sideways, crushed against the sarcophagus, barely able to move.

Seth.

The scarred red body of his hippo form forced the bricks from their mortar in the doorway until he filled the entire front wall of the crypt, flickering from moment to moment into the vile pig form that they recognised so easily, and the boy shape of Gouldian Finch; the eagle that had attacked Hathor; the secretary who had duped Jack and Albie – all guttering and spluttering into life as the four of them looked on in horror.

'You will not defeat me!' screeched a new form – a stinking slime of alligator scales covering a whale-sized body and a fanged snout that snapped above their heads, lower, closer, until they could feel burning saliva dripping onto their skin.

It was true. They could not defeat him. Not here, in this small space, with the element of surprise he had displayed so ably time after time …

But space and time were no longer constraints for Jack.

'Grandma Nut,' he cried, clutching everyone tighter. 'Now!'

And their reality - their now - shifted.

Chapter 21

At once, all together, they erupted into the throne room at the Field of Rushes. Jack immediately let go of his friends and ran to the vast doors that led back into the ballroom where he'd played many a game of basketball with his dead rellies.

He opened them quickly, reminded of the great hall in which Ozzy and Ice had been organising their festivities. It seemed so long ago that he could barely remember it, and yet it had only been days. 'Now. There is only now,' he reminded himself.

Poised in the doorway, he hollered into the ballroom.

'Everyone, I'm locking these doors. Seth is on the rampage! Take care.'

Panic ripped through the room, with spirits ancient and new gathering in groups to share war tactics. Jack was just about to close the doors and bolt them when he spotted a small straggle of people waving to him. It was Jay and Diselda, along with various people he'd introduced them to along the way, and a face that he was both shocked and somehow delighted to see – because he had rarely seen it looking so happy.

'Jackie,' said his father. 'They've just been telling me that it's you under that canine head. I can hardly bally-well believe it. Why didn't you just mention what you've been up to instead of making out you were an utter buffoon all this time?'

He didn't really know where to begin. Tell his father he was a dog-headed god? He thought it was weird enough that he didn't want to go to public school or wear a tie for dinner in the kitchen.

'Dad,' whispered Jack. 'Why ... you can't be here. I'm going to put your ba back in your body and send you back to Mum. I just—'

His father was shaking his head. 'No, you don't, son. I've always known there must be something great about you that I just couldn't see. Don't you get it? This is the natural order of things. I'm going to have a splendid time here. I'm already happier than I've been in decades. And you can just take over from me and look after your mother. You'll do a much better job than me anyway. I was always rubbish at it.'

'But I can't, Dad. I can't be a peer of the realm and run Lowmount.'

His father's heavy-handed spirit clapped him on the back. 'Nonsense. Look at what you're doing now. Good lord, is that Bone again?' he said suddenly, peering through the crack in the door. 'What's he doing here?'

'That's Albie, our very dear friend,' Jay interjected. 'And actually, Jack, what is he doing here?'

Granny Dazzle gazed at him, concerned. 'He isn't ... you know ... is he?'

'Ha! I always thought he might bat for the other side,' said Jackson darkly. 'No wife in all those years. Not natural.'

'No, not gay, Dad. Dead,' said Jack, wondering how much spirit counselling it would take for his father to lose all his many colourful prejudices, most of which seemed to be directed at Bone. 'Definitely not gay, because he's been in love with Granny Dazzle for practically his whole life.' Jay and Diselda both shrugged at Jackson. 'And no, not dead either. I just had hold of them all when I transported down here. Talking of which.' He nodded towards the throne room. 'I'd better bolt these doors.'

'You do that. I'm proud of you, Jack!' crowed Jackson, delighted with everyone and everything, especially his son.

Which was a first.

'Thanks, Dad,' said Jack softly, rather afraid he might start crying soon. His father – his old father – would never have countenanced that. 'And are you absolutely sure you want to stay?'

His father's eyes grew soft. 'I am. It's the way it's meant to be.' Then he straightened his shoulders. 'Now go and get the job done, my boy!'

'I will, Dad. I promise.'

Jack closed the doors and leaned his head against them for a second. In a series of surreal and unbelievable moments, the commendation from his father was perhaps the most surreal of all.

But there was no time to dwell on it, because Seth – who was also a father of his, of sorts, in the same way that Nephthys was a mother of his – would be upon them at any second.

Racing back to the others, he found Adjo and Minty standing with frowns on their faces before one of the tall chairs, while Albie pointed to another. This one he was familiar with.

'That's you!' hissed Albie.

'I know.'

'You're so lucky. This is amazing!'

Albie staggered around the throne room in tiny circles, lurching from one throne to the next, from a mural-covered wall to a table laden with artefacts, leaning back so that he could stare at the ceiling depicting the night sky, dappled with stars and a certain celestial dogstar.

'I can't believe I'm here. I can't believe it!' said Albie hoarsely, gripping Jack's arm.

'Neither can I. It was an accident. I didn't mean to bring any of you, but ... oh.'

Albie's insistent dragging had pulled him in front of the throne that Minty and Adjo had been inspecting. Jack had seen it before; he knew that if he gazed up at it, he would see the image of Osiris, indicating the seat that the pharaoh god would take in the ceremonial processing they undertook together.

But now Ozzy's face was gone. In its place was a younger face, with wide kohl-rimmed eyes that flicked at the corners – an eye that Jack had seen many months ago when Ozzy and Ice first led him to the museum. The eye of Horus.

'That's Horus,' Albie confirmed, not realising that it wasn't the reason Jack was shocked. His surprise was because it seemed Ozzy's replacement had already been selected. 'According to the mythology, Horus defeated Seth and ruled Egypt after Osiris, a young and noble leader who brought greatness back to the land.'

'But don't you see who it is?' whispered Jack.

Albie frowned. 'I just told you. It's Horus, depicted in so many hieroglyphs and likenesses that it's impossible to count.'

'I know, but –'

There was no time to explain what he had seen. What he now knew. It was confusing and astounding, but somehow inevitable …

Seth, however, was already here. Here in the throne room, a massive and brooding presence as a blood-red hippopotamus, but somehow even more terrifying when he appeared before them as Lord Set, thin-faced and feral, limping on the stump of a mis-shapen leg, driven to hideous and unthinkable murder by his ambition and greed. Ice and Nephthys, his own family, ran to remonstrate with him, but he pointed his crook at each of them in turn and blasted them through the heart.

Only it wasn't his crook. It was the Was Sceptre – Pharaoh's rod of his rule.

Minty and Adjo ran to help the goddesses, leaving Albie and Jack side by side and tremendously exposed in the centre of the enormous space. The nearest throne seemed to be miles away, and Jack felt Albie close in next to him.

'Get behind me,' he hissed.

Albie shivered but held fast. 'Nope. It we go down, we do it together. Joined by the same curse, remember?'

The sight ahead of them was nauseating. Seth opened his mouth as if he were unhinging his entire jaw, and from his gullet poured jet-black water that spread around the entire throne room, pooling around the legs of the great thrones and the people within it. As soon as the water touched a surface ... an object ... flesh, it thickened and solidified into a writhing mass of snakes.

'Yuck,' said Jack with a shudder.

'Asps,' Albie stated as if it were a swear word. 'I wish I had my naboot,' he continued. 'That could knock a few of these into kingdom come.'

'I remember, Kingdom Saver.'

Almost instinctively, Jack and Albie moved back to back. Jack also wished that Albie had his naboot with him – the stick with which he could do Egyptian martial arts – or that either of them had any kind of weapon.

Seth was striding towards them now, his sceptre parting the snakes like Moses separating the red sea. The ebony tide climbed to either side of him, snapping faces rising to within easy reach of a human neck, or even an inhuman one.

'Well,' said Albie with a sigh, 'it's been a tremendous honour, Jack. I haven't even minded being your servant.'

'You were never my servant, Alb. But you were always my friend.'

He felt Albie's shoulders droop slightly.

'Actually,' said Jack suddenly, watching Seth as they circled slowly, 'tell me again why you had to be our servant. What did that curse say?'

'Really? This is hardly the time to rub it in.'

'Humour me,' said Jack.

Ice was beginning to wail in the distance. It sounded less like crying and more like singing, a low mournful hymn that would gather her followers to her. Seth sensed triumph, his march speeding up.

Albie sighed, then shouted across the room. 'Remember this, Pig-face?

'In underworld, in afterlife,
Eternal torment, endless strife,
Never more to be undone
Until two true hearts beat as one.

Well, you did it! You bound us for life. Are you happy now?'

The sinister face of Lord Set split apart as the monster laughed triumphantly. Inky, poisonous green gases spurted from the open maw of his mouth. Jack covered his own mouth, spreading his arms wide to cover as much of Albie as he could. The singing was calling to him. Was that Ice again? Or a ringing in his ears. He couldn't work it out – that, or the questions in his mind. What did that rhyme mean? How could they end the curse? Who was the face on the throne? Why did Seth get to win? It wasn't fair! It just wasn't fair.

But then he realised what he was doing. He was looking for answers. And he couldn't find what was lost.

He had to empty his mind. Turning his head over his shoulder, he said loudly, 'So would you rather … go out with Minty, or be alone forever?'

'What?'

'Answer the question!'

'Oh. Well. Be alone forever, obviously.' He squirmed self-consciously.

'Okay, your turn.'

'Um, same question.'

Jack squirmed uneasily. 'Actually I've been thinking about asking Minty out.'

'You're kidding. She's a goddess!'

'I know.'

'No, I mean, she's an actual goddess. She can't go out with you. You're a mortal.'

'No, *you're* a mortal. She can't go out with you.'

Albie snorted furiously. 'I could go out with her if I wanted to. I think she likes me. She held my mortal hand very tight just now.'

'But I'm a god. Sort of.'

'True. Well, when are you going to ask her?'

'Don't know. If we survive this, I suppose.'

And in that moment, while he thought about the difficulties of asking out an actual goddess and wondered if they were going to survive, the information that had somehow got lost in his mind came to him in a blinding flash.

Seth was upon them, asps and poison spilling from his mouth and his fingertips. He raised the Was Sceptre above his head, reading to strike the forked crook of the staff into each of their faces, Albie first – the vulnerable one first.

Jack heard the singing, and to Seth's astonishment, he reached deep into the fork in the sceptre above him and drew out a metallic dagger that vibrated against his hand.

'That's mine,' he said with a grin. 'Remember?'

He slashed at Seth who staggered in shock, and although Jack hadn't damaged him at all, it was enough of a respite to enable him to wrench the staff from Seth's hand.

'Your naboot!' he cried to Albie.

Albie stared at it and then whooped happily. 'Amazing! That'll work!'

He shoved Seth in the stomach and he toppled backwards, into the seething mass of snakes that he himself had created. As he fell into them they disappeared and he righted himself instantly, flicking his insidious fingers at the tops of the thrones. One by one they began to waver and crash to the ground. Ice's. Thoth's. Jack's own. Any moment now the fourth, the one that had belonged to Ozzy but was now the seat of Horus, the new Pharaoh, would be quivering in the air directly over them. That face would descend, shattering their bodies as surely as Ozzy's had been broken up and scattered to the four winds.

It was the face of Seth's nemesis.

The throne began to fall, and Seth roared with delight as Jack's dagger and Albie's naboot flailed harmlessly towards him. Ice and Nephthys rallied to hold up the toppling throne, but their grip was tenuous, and Jack could see that they wouldn't be able to hold it for long. He lunged at Seth again, missing by an arm's length.

'Head of dog, you are as useless as a god as you are as a human,' he cried, barely able to conceal his joy at the prospect of ending their lives, their hold over him.

'I know that,' said Jack.

It was hearing the curse again that had finally made it clear to him. That, and the conversation with his two father figures – one who now had faith in him, and one who had none at all.

He – everyone – had always thought that the two hearts were the hearts of two different people.

Now, he knew the truth. Holding the dagger close to connect him to his grandmother, Nut, he asked what he needed to know. 'It's me, isn't it?'

And he felt, rather than heard her answer. Yes.

Of course. All this time he'd been trying to be normal – not a lord, but someone ordinary. But denying that he was destined to own a castle was as pointless as denying that he was some kind of demi-god. The evidence was all there, all around him. He was very far from ordinary. He had two highly unusual jobs to do, two highly unusual sets of parents and god-parents. And furthermore, people relied on him – for both roles.

'You know what?' he said aloud, jabbing at Seth half-heartedly to buy some time to speak. 'I may be useless as a god and also as a human, but if I'm both of those things, all the time – and I know that I am – then I'm pretty invincible. All this time, I've thought I wanted to be just an ordinary teenager. I've rejected this doghead and what it makes me do. But now I know it's part of me. I embrace it. Both halves of me.'

Suddenly he stood tall, a surge of power run through him such as he'd never experienced before. 'I'm Jackanubis!' he cried. 'And my two hearts beat as one!'

He felt it too – the hum of the lantern within him synchronising with the thump of his human heart. A blast of searing light filled the room, and Jack experienced a sensation of complete invincibility. 'I'm Jackanubis!' he howled joyfully.

'Dear chap, I think you've lost it,' muttered Albie.

'We'll see. Do you still feel like my servant?'

Albie went to punch him, and connected. 'No!' he said, astonished. 'Sorry.'

'Never mind!'

Behind them – close behind them – he heard the sound of two hands high-fiving, and suddenly a hawk flew overhead. Hathor. It must be Minty and Adjo sneaking through the murky mist to join them.

If he didn't sort this out soon, they'd be joining them under the falling edifice of the Horus throne.

Seth, meanwhile, had not realised that his advantage was lost. 'That curse matters no longer, Head of Dog. You can never defeat me!'

Jack hesitated, watching the face on the throne descend as the goddesses grappled to keep their grip. It was a face that had become very familiar.

'No, maybe I can't,' he said calmly. 'But he can.'

And in the same moment as he pointed up at the image of Horus on the throne, he pushed his dagger backwards through the mist.

'Adjo. Take him!'

'Of course!'

The wise old soul encompassed in a young, strong body slid forward without a moment's hesitation. In one smooth movement, Adjo seized the dagger and pushed himself past a stunned Albie, the boy king's wide eyes brimming with honour and pride.

Then he leapt to his feet, rising from the mist like a spirit before Seth who, in his ignorance, was still watching Jack. The dagger flashed across Seth's body in two clean strikes.

The pig eyes that were staring at Jack widened, startled and outraged, as pungent green smoke poured from the cuts across Seth's chest. Higher and higher it rose, leaking into their throats, drowning them as if it was the water of the Nile itself. Then suddenly the liquid seeping from the slashes in Seth's body turned into scarlet droplets. The evil light in Seth's eyes gleamed as he reached a hand out incredulously. Blood. The liquid dripping from his chest was blood. Suddenly confused, the eyes narrowed and then dulled ... and then finally, as the body slumped to the floor, they snapped shut.

A stunned silence followed – a silence that was broken by the creak of the felled throne as it sawed through the air towards them. Catching hold of Albie and Adjo, Jack Zipped to the doorway to the ballroom, appearing next to Minty as the enormous seat crashed to the floor, crushing whatever remained of the terrible Lord Set.

Seth was gone.

The curse was gone.

They were finally – finally – free.

And yet Jack, for some unknown reason, felt terribly alone.

Chapter 22

Jack's fears and feelings of desolation seemed to be justified, too.

It started, of course, with Adjo. In the aftermath of the Battle of the Throne Room, as the rellies insisted on calling it, the four younger participants had watched in awe as Ice and Nephthys drew it all back together, sweeping away all remnants of Seth on a cleansing tide that cascaded in a waterfall down one wall and whooshed out through the open doors across the Field of Rushes, resurrecting thrones as if they were doing origami on a massive scale.

Then Ice called Adjo to her side. 'You have done well, young man. Well you have done.'

'Thank you!' said Adjo, affable as ever.

'Would it bring you any regret if, rather than returning as a boy to the bazaar, you were to follow in Osiris' footsteps, ruling this great nation fairly, wisely and abundantly?'

Adjo erupted into peals of laughter. 'Me? A poor souk shoe seller? No, it would bring me no regret. I have had the chance to see my family again, and that is all I wished for. But I am too lowly.'

'If I may interject, madam,' said Albie formally, 'I can confirm that he truly is a wise and considerate soul. He's counselled me through many an issue, and is as insightful as he is energetic.'

Jack held up a hand. 'And he's a genius at inventing things! Look at the way he got Ozzy back to the crypt.'

'He truly is,' agreed Albie.

'Then he will be a great leader, casting a soulful eye across all of Egypt.'

His coronation, of course, was to be at the palace in Thebes, so they said their goodbyes in the ballroom. 'I cannot thank you enough,' said Adjo. 'I am blessed beyond all reason. Ra in you!' he squeaked deliriously.

Jack, Albie and Minty all laughed. 'And in you,' they replied together.

Then he pressed his forehead to their hands and finally waved frantically with tears in his luminous dark eyes.

'I'm going to miss him,' said Albie.

'Well, I'm not.' Minty folded her arms defensively.

Jack and Albie stared at each other and then at Minty. 'Don't you like him?' said Jack.

'No, that's not what I mean.' Looking very uncomfortable, Minty huffed out a deep breath. 'I mean that I won't have to miss him, because I'm going with him.'

Jack's heart plummeted for the umpteenth time that week.

'Why?' he said, a little too loudly. 'Do you have to?'

'No, I don't have to, but I want to. Nephthys sent me to watch over you, Jack, and you don't need me any longer.'

'I do,' he bleated, kicking himself but unable to stop.

'Adjo – Horus needs me now, at least for a while,' said Minty with a laugh. 'And that's the life I'm really used to. I've missed it.'

Albie grinned at Jack's forlorn face. 'He was going to ask you out.'

'I heard,' said Minty, pointing at Hathor.

Jack flushed to the tips of his ears. 'Well, that's not embarrassing at all.'

'You are still a boy at heart, and I need an ancient heart and mind of knowledge. I thought there was someone … but it is not to be. And it is not our time, Jackanubis.'

But I thought our time was NOW, he wanted to shout. Why are you going off with Adjo? Then he realised he was being a bit sulky about the whole thing, so he gave her a hug.

Albie deliberately and politely shook her hand, then on the very last second he abruptly pressed it to his lips as Jay had done in the souk.

'Nice job, Amentet,' he said formally, but Jack noticed his friend was trying not to sniff as she vanished into the Field of Rushes with Nephthys and Adjo.

Which left Ice, Albie and himself.

'So are we going home now?' he said to Albie hopefully. He knew he could massage time and all that, and that difficult moments lay ahead what with his father still insisting on staying in the underworld, but he suddenly thought it might be quite nice to get back to a bit of normality. Not normal normality, but a new normality in which he was half man, half dog-god, and sometimes both at once.

But then the unimaginable happened.

Albie shook his head.

'Do I have a choice as to where I go ... and when?' he asked hesitantly, more to Ice than to Jack.

'You are no longer bound, and the choice is yours,' said the goddess.

Jack gazed at him. 'But where would you go apart from Lowmount? It's been your home for ... like ... centuries! With us. With me!'

'But that's just it, Jack.' Albie stared at his shoes, searching for words. 'It was your home – the Bootle-Cadogans. I had to be there because of the curse. I never really got the chance to find out where my home was, or who I might have ended up with. I might have had a family of my own, and ... well, I think I'd really like to take a crack at being that world-famous archaeologist I always wanted to be.'

'Huh. But who's going to help me mummify the locals?'

Albie laughed, then shrugged. 'Who knows what will happen now? There might be nobody to mummify.'

'There's my father,' said Jack, but then he realised he would probably be the last person Albie would want to assist into a smooth and lovely afterlife.

'I will help you with your father, Jackanubis,' said Ice kindly. 'Help you I will. After I've dropped Albie off in …'

'Luxor,' said Albie. 'In 1922. No! 1921. Then hopefully I will avoid running into Jay and Diselda until I've sorted a few things out for myself.'

'As is your will,' said Ice.

What about my will? Jack wanted to shout. Why's everybody leaving?

But he knew the answer in the depths of his twin hearts. It was their 'now'. Each of his friends were free to return to the path they would have been on without Seth's curse. They could all relive their now.

With a sombre nod, Jack extended his hand to Albie, thumb up and his palm spread wide. Albie clutched it without a second thought, then pulled Jack in for a hug.

'You'll hear from me again, old boy,' said Albie hoarsely.

'I'd better. And not in mime, okay?'

'Okay.'

Saying goodbye seemed impossible, so they didn't really. Jack gave Albie his dagger, and told him to "find" it somewhere special.

'It's made of meteorite,' he told him, 'and it explains a whole lot about the pyramids and so on. Focus on the dogstar, Sirius.'

Then he'd taken pity on him and described the starfield and his visit to meet his grandmother, Nut.

'See, that's what I mean,' said Albie. 'I never got to meet my own grandmother.'

'Well, I'm pretty sure she wasn't a goddess or an alien.'

'You just never know,' said Albie darkly.

Then he raised the dagger in a salute to Jack, shielding his spectacles from the glare as Ice directed the disk on her headdress towards him, till the light reflected all around the Bootle-Cadogan family's oldest friend ...

What he did after that, Jack didn't know, because he'd closed his eyes at that point. When he opened them again, he was back in the crypt. He looked around hopefully for Albie, or Jay, or even Claire the National Trust lady, but it was hideously empty.

Rather like his chest.

Deeply sad, he'd trudged along the corridor to the museum, seeing memories in every dust particle: the eye of Horus on the back of the door; the camp bed on which Ozzy 'n' Ice had travelled across Hampshire; Granny Dazzle's impressive suitcase in which he'd found the instruments of mummification.

That had all been several weeks ago, however, and since then Jack had found the business of becoming a lord and dealing with funerals far less fun that being a god and dealing with mummification. His mother was weepy at the best of times and silently brooding at the worst, and he could only begin to imagine how she felt when he himself expected to hear his father ranting at every turn in the corridor.

They'd managed to have one fairly nice morning, when Jack visited the greenhouses for the very first time in his life to help his mother pick out flowers for the chapel.

'You'll have to make a speech, you know. The new Lord Bootle-Cadogan and so on.'

'I know. I'm already working on it.'

'Jack! Listen to you! You're not balking at the prospect of being a lord.'

'I've accepted it,' said Jack casually. 'It's part of me, and I'll just have to get on with it.'

'That's just what your father would say!' Lady BC snapped a rose from its stem and buried her nose in it. 'This one. Your father's favourite.'

'Dad had a favourite flower?'

'A favourite rose. Peonies were his favourite flower.'

Wow. There really was so much that he didn't know about his own father. They'd never really got beyond the stage of sniping at each other over school reports.

And talking of school …

'I've been thinking, Mum,' he said, trailing behind her as she plonked mounds of vegetation into his arms. 'You know Dad always wanted me to go to Eton, and I always insisted on going to Clearwell Comp?'

His mother whisked around. 'Oh, Jack. Have you changed your mind? Are you going to go to Eton in honour of your father's memory?'

'Actually, no.' Jack watched his mother's eyes flood with disappointed tears and revved up his speech. 'But I have been wondering if there's a … well, a third option. We've got this massive castle with all these spare rooms apart from over the summer holiday when they're holiday lets, and it might be good to give people who don't … you know … fit in anywhere else a place that they might learn. About stuff.'

He couldn't really tell her much of his plans. What could he say: 'I'd like to find other people more like me, who live between worlds or are unusual in some ways. I've run it all past Granny Dazzle who still hangs out in the crypt on occasions, and the other grandma who lives in my chest stroke on another planet. Take your pick, Mum!'

Instead he just smiled hopefully.

'Well, I suppose we could think about it,' said his mother, frowning. 'I'm sure I don't know how we're going to run this godforsaken mausoleum of a place if we don't do something inventive with it.'

'Exactly.'

'And what might this school be called?'

Jack grinned. 'I've already thought of that. How about … the School of ICE? That stands for Inter-Connecting Energies, and it also represents, well, an old friend of mine.'

'Oh, Jack. Your father would …' His mother paused in her ramblings to place a hand on each of his shoulders. '… absolutely bally hate that.'

But she hadn't said no, and Jack was encouraged by that. At least it was something to focus on, while he wondered why he was the only one left in this godforsaken mausoleum of a place.

And here he was again, back in the chapel for a funeral, and not for his great grandmother this time, but his own father. At Granny Dazzle's funeral he had played Copa Cobana on a CD player, but for this occasion his mother had rolled in a chamber orchestra who played some dismal dirges that were also, apparently, favourites of his father's.

He'd ask him later. One day. He was bound to start turning up in the crypt for chats soon, and if not, Jack could Zip down the Underworld and join him for a few rounds of god-golf. It was a very handy part of the fact that he had embraced his inner Anubis.

When it was time for his speech, he gave a simple eulogy to his father, and mentioned what an honour it was to be following in such esteemed footsteps.

'He cared a lot about Lowmount and his family, and I want to be sure that I do the same when – now – that I'm Lord Bootle-Cadogan. I would like to think Dad would be proud of me.'

Then he joined the other pallbearers beneath the coffin, wishing he could transform and carry it on his own. It was his father, after all. And he was strong enough alone – it seemed a shame to have these gifts and not use them.

The coffin was lowered into the grave, with nobody but Jack and a mysterious blue-eyed visitor called Ice knowing that, beneath its lid and above its copper bottom, lay a carefully mummified body with an array of special objects around it, including a fabric peony and an old dog tag of Roger's.

Finally, as it was drawing to a close, Jack dared to heave in a deep breath and look around him. Soon they would make their way up to the kitchen where they'd broken with the tradition of a standard wake to lay out a simple supper of beef and ale pie and mash – just the kind of meal his father would have adored.

After that, he'd sit with his mum until she wanted to be on her own or she dropped off, and then he'd roam the castle on his own as he did every night. Looking. Waiting. Always half-expecting that one of his friends would turn up.

As he glanced at the assembled mourners near the famous tamarisk tree, a very unusual sight met his eyes. Jack's heart lurched.

Beneath the tree was a sheep, and beside it, a pair of tethered goats who butted each other with mutual levels of disgust and violence.

It was just like Granny Dazzle's funeral.

Jack hopped from one foot to the other throughout the tail end of the service, anxiously waiting for it to be over. 'I'll run back to the castle,' he whispered to his mother as the cars drew up – Bonelessly, of course – to drive them home. 'I need the fresh air.'

She didn't protest, but simply pressed her forehead against his for a second or two, then sucked in a deep breath and made her way to the car.

He waved her off, making running motions that would have made Bone proud.

Once he was alone, instead of heading towards the turrets and towers of his distant home, Jack pelted over to the tree and checked behind the goats. As he'd suspected – hoped? – a number of items were piled up there.

He checked them off the list in his head, still remembered from last time:

Two sycamore logs.
Eight small sheets of copper.
Plus two goats and a sheep.

Then he heard shuffling from further behind the tree, and a voice saying, 'I told you!'

Jack stuck his head around the trunk. Scrunched up in the bracken at the base of the tree was a couple – or at least, one male and one female, approximately his age, with dark skin and eyes. The girl wore slender glasses, while the boy squinted at him in a manner that told Jack he needed them too but was too vain to wear them.

They both stood up slowly.

'I *told* you,' muttered the girl again.

'You told him what?'

'I told him you were coming over. We just wanted to make sure the goats didn't escape.' The girl sighed. 'We didn't expect you to actually WALK across.'

The boy pulled a guilty face. 'It was just supposed to be a joke, anyway – but then it seemed kind of mean when we saw the funeral going on. Sorry.'

'Why?' said Jack abruptly.

They looked at each other. 'Well, because it's clearly for someone you're close to and you look sad,' explained the girl, who appeared to be the more feisty of the pair.

'No, I wasn't asking why you were sorry. I was asking why you left these things here – these particular things – as a joke.'

'Ah,' said the boy, as the girl slid her spectacles up her nose in a way that Jack recognised from somewhere. 'Our dad made us do it, because his grandad was always going on about the massive connections with Egypt at this place called Lowmount, and if we ever heard of a funeral going on we should deliver – well, this stuff.'

'We're just staying nearby and thought it would be funny when we heard about today, but now … oh, it just looks cruel.' The girl held up her hands. 'Look, we're really, really sorry.'

'It's okay,' said Jack, his mind racing. 'And your great grandfather was interested in Egypt, was he?'

They both laughed at the same moment, and Jack suddenly realised that they were twins. 'Totally obsessed!'

cried the girl. 'He was this famous archaeologist in about 1920. Found the lost grave of Os... Oz someone or other.'

Jack nodded slowly, hardly able to stop himself from running over and hugging the pair of them.

'This is him, with our great grandmother,' said the boy, passing him a clipping from an old newspaper.

His old friend – very old, though not in this picture – stood triumphantly beside a coffin in the desert, smiling down at his shiny-haired wife. Blimey! He said he could never love another woman – and he hadn't, because his wife was a goddess.

So he actually did want to ask Minty out, thought Jack. And when he'd assumed that Minty was going to pair up with Adjo, she'd actually been looking for a different ancient heart. For some reason, he was incredibly pleased. They belonged together in a way that he and Minty never would have done.

'I know about that guy. Albie – Albert Cornthwaite.'

'Yes! Wow, he was obviously right about the Egypt connections here. Nobody knows his name usually, unless they're a complete nerd.'

'I'm a complete nerd,' said Jack with a grin. Then he stuck out his hand in a fashion that would have made Albie proud. 'Lord Bootle-Cadogan!' he said. 'But call me Jack.'

'I'm Joe,' said the boy, and he flipped his head towards his sister. 'She's Mindy.'

Of course you are, thought Jack. 'Very, very pleased to meet you both. Look, you've obviously been crouched there for ages. There's some food up at the hall. Would you like to join us?'

They agreed, delighted, chatting all the way back to the castle.

'So how long are you staying nearby?' said Jack as they rounded the ornamental fountain.

'Maybe a long time.' Mindy grinned at him. 'If our parents can find a decent school.'

'One that will have us.' Joe laughed, which suddenly turned into a sneezing fit. Immediately, a tiny cloud shot into position above his head and scattered raindrops onto his hair. 'Eugh,' he said quickly, trying to avoid his sister's eye as she glared murderously at him. 'Think it's going to rain.'

'Maybe,' said Jack. 'Or maybe not. You'll be fine, here, whichever it is.'

And Jack threw open the kitchen door to be greeted by the enticing aroma of slow-cooked beef and creamy mash.

It was all going to be okay.

No, not going to be. Now.

It was all very, very much okay.

'Welcome to Lowmount,' he said.

The End

ABOUT THE AUTHOR

Jill Marshall is a proud mum, nana and communications consultant, as well as the author of dozens of books for children, young adults and (old) adults. When she's not doing any of those things, she loves singing, dancing and theatre and going to see other people do singing, dancing and theatre. She divides her time between the UK and New Zealand, and hopes one day to travel between the two by SatiSPI.

Look out for rest of the Jack B-C trilogy:

DOGHEAD

and

DOGFIGHT

Also featuring Jack -

S*W*A*G*G 1, Spook

Want the full SWAGG experience?

Immerse yourself in the origin stories.

The Jane Blonde series
Jane Blonde, Sensational Spylet
Jane Blonde Spies Trouble
Jane Blonde, Twice the Spylet
Jane Blonde, Spylet on Ice
Jane Blonde, Goldenspy
Jane Blonde, Spy in the Sky
Jane Blonde, Spylets are Forever

Jack BC in the Doghead trilogy
1 Jack BC, Doghead
2. Jack BC, Dogfight
3. Jack BC, Dogstar

The Legend of Matilda Peppercorn
TLOMP, Witch Hunter
TLOMP, Toadstone
TLOMP, Questioner
TLOMP, Trinity

Stein & Frank:
Battle of the Undead People-Eaters

Also by Jill Marshall
Available in print, mobi, epub and audio.

For Young Adults
Pineapple
Fanmail
Lena's Fortune

For Adults
The Most Beautiful Man in the World
The Two Miss Parsons
As It Is on Telly

For younger children
Kave-Tina Rox

For more adventures and information,

visit www.jillmarshallbooks.com

Follow Jill Marshall Books on Facebook

Email jill on info@jillmarshallbooks.com

www.ingramcontent.com/pod-product-compliance
Lightning Source LLC
Chambersburg PA
CBHW010824070526
44583CB00022B/2928